GRACE
REVOLUTION

STUDY GUIDE

ALSO BY JOSEPH PRINCE

Grace Revolution

Glorious Grace

Reign in Life

The Power of Right Believing

100 Days of Right Believing

Destined To Reign

Destined To Reign Devotional

Unmerited Favor

100 Days of Favor

Healing Promises

Provision Promises

Health And Wholeness Through The Holy Communion

A Life Worth Living

The Benjamin Generation

Your Miracle Is In Your Mouth

Right Place Right Time

Spiritual Warfare

For more information on these books and other inspiring resources, visit JosephPrince.com.

JOSEPH PRINCE

GRACE REVOLUTION

STUDY GUIDE

Experience the power to live above defeat

New York | Boston | Nashville

All Scripture quotations, unless otherwise indicated, are taken from the New King James Version. Copyright © 1982 by Thomas Nelson, Inc. Used by permission. All rights reserved.

Scripture quotations marked AMP are taken from the Amplified Bible. Copyright © 1954, 1958, 1962, 1964, 1965, 1987 by The Lockman Foundation. Used by permission.

Scripture quotations marked KJV are from the King James Version of the Bible.

Scripture quotations marked NASB are from the New American Standard Bible. Copyright © 1960, 1962, 1963, 1968, 1971, 1972, 1973, 1975, 1977, 1995 by The Lockman Foundation. Used by permission. (www.lockman.org)

Scripture quotations marked NIV are taken from the Holy Bible, New International Version, NIV. Copyright © 1973, 1978, 1984, 2011 by Biblica, Inc. Used by permission of Zondervan. All rights reserved worldwide. (www.zondervan.com)

Scripture quotations marked NLT are taken from the Holy Bible, New Living Translation. Copyright © 1996, 2004, 2007. Used by permission of Tyndale House Publishers, Inc, Carol Stream, Illinois 60188. All rights reserved.

FaithWords
Hachette Book Group
1290 Avenue of the Americas
New York, NY 10104
www.faithwords.com

Printed in the United States of America

First Edition: April 2016
10 9 8 7 6 5 4 3 2 1

FaithWords is a division of Hachette Book Group, Inc.
The FaithWords name and logo are trademarks of Hachette Book Group, Inc.

The Hachette Speakers Bureau provides a wide range of authors for speaking events. To find out more, go to www.hachettespeakersbureau.com or call (866) 376-6591.

The publisher is not responsible for websites (or their content) that are not owned by the publisher.

ISBN: 978-1-45559-586-0

CONTENTS

INTRODUCTION

I'm delighted that you've chosen to use this study guide that was written as a companion to my book, *Grace Revolution: Experience the Power to Live Above Defeat.* This study guide will help establish you in the gospel of grace so that you experience lasting breakthroughs in every area of your life.

My dear reader, it's no coincidence that you've picked up this study guide. I prayed that this book would find its way to the right person at the right time!

I believe that the thoughts and questions you'll find in the following pages will help you establish a deeper understanding of the glorious person of Christ and His gospel of grace and launch you toward developing right beliefs about God's love and grace toward you that will bring hope, confidence, joy, and lasting inside-out transformation to every practical area of life.

My friend, if you are going through a severe challenge in your life, know that God is right now reaching out to you in love with His Word of grace. He knows all about it and He just wants you to lean your full weight on His love, and allow Him to work deeply in you and turn your situation around.

I really believe that God has truths for you in this book that will empower you to live above defeat, as well as build an unshakable, rock-solid foundation upon which you can enjoy a life of peace, health, and victory!

This study guide has been created so that it lends itself to both self-study or personal development, as well as small-group study or discussion, say in a care group or book club setting. Whichever the purpose you have in mind, you'll find ample opportunity to personally encounter the Lord as you take time to study and meditate on His Word, and hear His Spirit speak and minister His grace to your heart and mind.

The format of each chapter is simple and user-friendly. To get the most out of each chapter, it would be best to first read the corresponding chapter in the parent book (*Grace Revolution*). That'll give you more background and understanding. If you're not sure how to answer a certain question that is based on a teaching in the parent book, there's a helpful answer guide at the back you can refer to. It covers all the questions except for those that require a personal response from you.

If you decide to use this study guide in a small-group setting, a good habit is to do some preparation before each meeting. Take some time to read the relevant portions of text and to reflect on the questions and how they apply to you. This will give your group study depth and make the sessions much more fruitful and productive for all.

Because of the personal nature of this study guide, if you do use it in a group setting, remember to keep any sensitive or personal content that is shared within the group! Confidentiality, courtesy, and mutual respect lay the foundation for a healthy, safe group. Commit yourself to listening in love to your fellow participants, encouraging each other in the revelation of the Scriptures and of the gospel that you are discovering together, and show each participant the grace that this study is all about.

Beloved, whether in personal study or with a group, I am believing with you that each session will be most inspiring, and take you to a whole new level of faith, strength, wholeness, and victory in Christ!

KEY 1

GROW IN BOLDNESS AND CONFIDENCE

CHAPTER 1

LET THE REVOLUTION BEGIN

My friend, a grace revolution is sweeping across the world today and it's transforming precious lives, restoring broken marriages, healing the sick, and freeing many from their long-term conditions, addictions, and the bondage of legalism. There is one common denominator that tipped these people over from defeat into victory, from breakdowns into breakthroughs: they all had *an encounter with Jesus*. They all caught a revelation of His grace.

Grace is not a subject and the grace revolution is not a movement. Grace is a person and His name is Jesus. No matter where you are at or what challenges you face, the positive changes you want to see begin to happen when you *know* and *believe* in the person of Jesus and the perfection of His finished work. When your heart and mind are anchored on His grace and the power of His finished work in your life, *He* will transform you from the inside out. When you personally encounter Him and allow your mind to be renewed with right beliefs about your true identity in Him, you will walk in freedom and live life to the fullest!

1. **What you believe about Jesus makes all the difference. Take a moment to write down who He is to you. Describe what your encounter with Jesus to date has been like.**

The grace revolution is about your life transformed from the inside out. It is about a life that reigns triumphant over defeat, failure, and frustration. When you encounter Jesus, the person of grace, see His heart of love for you, and when the veil of Christian religion is removed, you begin to step away from defeat and take a massive leap toward your victory!

Read Dean's amazing testimony (page 4 of *Grace Revolution*). In it, he describes how feelings of rejection, inadequacy, loneliness, and fear launched him into a life of addictions and bondage, how his beliefs about God kept him trapped in defeat for over thirty years as he struggled with his addictions, and how his turnaround happened only when he began to hear about God's grace.

2. **What did Dean discover about God's grace and the love of Jesus for him that started him on his journey to freedom?**

3. **Why did that make such an impact on him? What did he believe about God at that time?**

4. **What more did Dean discover about the "simplicity of the gospel of Christ" that began to transform him "from the inside out" and that brought him to a place of effortless change?**

The last paragraph of Dean's praise report shows us that no matter how defeated or hopeless we feel, a growing revelation of God's grace can turn that situation around and bring true deliverance.

5. **What is the message of hope from Dean's story that you feel God is personally speaking to your heart as you consider your own challenges?**

As was the case with Dean, many believers are still living in confusion. They believe God will bless them when they obey Him, and then curse them when they fall short and fail. They get law and grace all mixed up by holding on to some aspects of the law and some aspects of grace in their Christian walk. Jesus said you cannot put new wine into old wineskins. The new wine will ferment and break the wineskins, and you will lose both (see Matt. 9:17). In the same way, you cannot put the new wine of grace into the old wineskin of the law. The result, as Dean shared about his life, is one of guilt, shame, bone-crushing condemnation, and depression because of fear, failure, and punishment.

Confusing law and grace is dangerous because it nullifies the finished work of Jesus . . . The law is man-centered whereas grace is Jesus-centered. The law focuses on what you must accomplish; grace focuses entirely on what Jesus has accomplished. Under the law, you are disqualified by your disobedience; under grace, you are qualified by Jesus' obedience. Under the law you are made righteous when you do right; under grace you are made righteous when you believe right.

Read pages 10 and 11 which sum up the differences between living under the law and living under grace. Now consider the table below and fill out the column under grace.

UNDER LAW	UNDER GRACE
My focus is on what I need to accomplish for God	
I am disqualified by my disobedience	
I am made righteous (or justi-fied) only by my works/only when I do right	
I am constantly demand-conscious, because the law demands righteousness from me	

The truth is, through the cross at Calvary, all who believe in Jesus and acknowledge Him as their Lord and Savior are under the new covenant of grace. This is what Jesus' finished work has accomplished for you. He died for you so that you can now come *completely* under God's grace and experience the breakthroughs you need.

6. **How do you feel, knowing that our Lord Jesus through His finished work has set you free from the demands of the law and put you completely under God's grace? Take a moment to give thanks to the Lord and share with Him how this blesses you.**

When Jesus preached the Sermon on the Mount, He brought the law back to its pristine standard, as the Pharisees had brought it down to where it was humanly possible to keep. He did this to show that it was impossible for man to be justified by the law. Jesus was using God's law to bring man to the end of himself so that he will see his need for the Savior.

The good news is that Jesus preached God's holy standards in the Sermon of the Mount, and then He came down the mountain to meet the needs of suffering, crying, and dying humanity. If Jesus had stayed high up in heaven and decreed God's holy standards from there, there would have been no hope and no redemption for us. But He came down the mountain and met a man with leprosy, a picture of you and me before we were washed clean by His precious blood. Imagine: an unclean sinner, standing before the King of kings. There was no way the pristine and perfect standards of the Sermon on the Mount or of God's holy commandments could have saved him or us. The King knew that and that's why He came down to where we were.

So here the man with leprosy was before the King saying, "Lord, if You are willing, You can make me clean" (Matt. 8:2). Our Lord Jesus reached out and *touched* the defiled man, saying, "I am willing; be cleansed." And immediately his leprosy was cleansed (see Matt. 8:3). Now watch this: under the law those with leprosy—the unclean—make the clean unclean. But under grace Jesus makes the unclean clean!

7. **How does knowing that "the King came down" and has the power to make the unclean, clean, give you hope in the midst of your challenges?**

There are people who twist God's Word, saying that when people are under grace, it will cause them to sin without restraint. Many have been hoodwinked by this false teaching that makes people fearful of God's grace. Nothing could be further from the truth. It is being under grace that gives you the power to live a victorious life. Romans 6:14 clearly states: "For sin shall not have dominion over you, for you are not under law but under grace." The word "sin" here means "a failing to hit the mark." So you can say it this way: sicknesses, diseases, eating disorders, addictions, and any form of oppression or bondage (all examples of our missing God's mark or standard for a glorious life) shall not have dominion over you. When? When you are not under the law but under grace!

8. **Would you like to have power over sin in your life, instead of living under sin's dominion? According to Romans 6:14, when and how can this be a reality?**

9. After reading this chapter, and particularly Anna's amazing testimony, what did you discover about Jesus and His love for you?

Toward the end of her testimony, Anna said, "Even right now, thinking about this great freedom, I have to cry, and cry out, 'My Father is SO faithful!' . . . I am so grateful that Christ has set me free!"

What willpower and self-effort couldn't do, God did by the power of His amazing grace. His living and eternal Word proclaims, "For sin shall not have dominion over you, for you are not under law but under grace" (Rom. 6:14). Grace is the power over every addiction that is destroying you. Only grace can give you lasting freedom.

10. Do you really believe that it is God's heart to set you free of every kind of defeat and give you lasting freedom? Write a prayer to the Lord, telling Him how you feel as you reflect on this truth, and thank Him for His grace that overcomes everything destructive in your life.

CHAPTER 2

INSIDE-OUT TRANSFORMATION

The grace revolution is about the inside-out transformation that occurs in the innermost sanctum of the human heart when a person encounters Jesus and His grace personally. We see this played out in the fisherman Peter's first meeting with Jesus. Peter had returned to shore with empty nets when Jesus met him, asked to get into his boat . . . and gave him a net-breaking, boat-sinking load of fish. Read this account (see pages 18–20), paying careful attention to Peter's response to Jesus' words to let down the nets, and then his response to Jesus after his unprecedented catch.

1. What was Peter's reaction to Jesus when so many large fish rushed into the net that it began to tear from the unprecedented load?

2. Which came first—Peter's repentance or God's blessing? What does that tell you about the new covenant of grace?

3. Some people think they must first sort their lives out before they can come to Jesus and ask for His help. What is the problem with this thinking?

Many people get confused when they are told to "repent" of their sins. To help you understand, on page 23 of *Grace Revolution*, I showed you something beautiful hidden in the Hebrew word for repentance, *teshuvah*, that shows God's heart and explanation of what true repentance is. Read that section again, but slowly this time.

4. Putting it all together, what does *teshuvah* mean? What is repentance all about?

5. So if someone makes a mistake or is struggling with a sinful habit and feels a sense of shame, how does he practice true repentance as opposed to the kind of repentance that puts many believers under bondage?

Don't run away from God. Run *to* Him! He is your Savior. He is your solution and your answer. He loves you and wants to love you into wholeness and transform you with His perfect love.

6. Having established that repentance is returning to God's grace because of the cross, how does that change your thoughts about repentance and about how God wants you to relate to Him?

Sin is destructive and brings with it many damaging consequences. Some ministers think that when there is sin, they need to preach stronger, harder, and harsher sermons on the law of Moses. But the Word of God tells us that "the strength of sin is the law" (1 Cor. 15:56). Preaching more law is like adding more fuel to the fire. Beating people down with the law of Moses doesn't liberate and transform them.

7. Based upon Romans 6:14, what is the only scriptural way for a person to be liberated from the power of sin and transformed from the inside-out?

Living under grace unlocks the power of God to overcome every sin.

We looked at the Hebrew word for repentance. Now let's look at the Greek word for repentance—*metanoia*. *Meta* means "change," while *noia* is from the word *nous*, which means "mind." So *metanoia* or repentance means "a change of mind." Why is changing your mind important? Simply because right believing always leads to right living.

When you believe right about God's grace, about your righteousness in Christ, and how you are called to be set apart for holiness, everything changes! His love touches you in the deepest recesses of your heart and you begin to experience transformation from the inside out. That's the grace revolution in action. You begin to live above defeat and experience lasting breakthroughs because the power to fight off any temptation is not from without, but from within. It is not contingent upon your willpower; it is contingent upon the power of the Holy Spirit living mightily in you, bearing witness to the gospel truths you believe.

8. **If a believer is looking for a way out of some bad habit or addiction, what happens when he believes right (believes the truth) about God's grace and love toward him? Will it strengthen his desire to sin or give him an excuse to sin, as some claim?**

In Robert's testimony of how he confessed his fifteen-year addiction to spit tobacco in front of his church and resolved to stop, he noted that within a week he was back at it and feeling great condemnation (see pages 27 and 28 of *Grace Revolution*). Although he said, "I fought and fought, quit and quit, over and over again," his attempts to "repent" and change didn't work and made it worse.

9. **What truth did Robert hear that finally set him free?**

10. **After hearing and receiving a revelation of the gospel, how did Robert respond whenever he felt the urge for tobacco?**

11. **As is true of most believers, Robert thought that to overcome a sin, weakness, or addiction he had to "feel remorse and repent" through his own willpower. How is your learning of what true repentance is stirring up faith and a renewed sense of hope in you?**

Robert found freedom and the power to stay on an *upward cycle of victory*. Real change happened when he discovered the truth of God's grace, what the Lord Jesus has done for him on the cross, and how God still loves him and would help him despite his failings. And as he began to *focus* on these truths and *return* to these truths of God's grace every time he felt an urge to return to his habit, he began to experience victory over his addiction.

This is what believing right—true repentance—did for Robert. The right living Robert wanted to experience became a reality not when he was trying to make it happen on his own, but when he discovered and then kept returning to grace whenever he was weak. This is the key to overcoming sin and every bondage in your life.

12. Do you desire to experience this upward cycle of victory? How can you start to make this lasting transformation a reality in your life today?

As we end our study of this chapter, know that God wants you to return to the person of grace and His finished work every time you feel weak or fail. It will always bring deliverance, a fresh start, and new ways of living and loving that will radically transform your life.

CHAPTER 3

HEAR THE WORD OF HIS GRACE

In Jesus' day, those with leprosy were ostracized and isolated in accordance with the law of Moses. Because they were conscious of how unclean they were and that violations of the law were punishable by stoning, their natural response was to withdraw and hide.

One such man with leprosy had hidden himself beneath a stone slab on the Mount of Beatitudes for fear of being seen by the gathering crowd. He had come to hear the man they called "Jesus," whom others said healed all who came to Him, no matter what their conditions. *All.* That little word gave him hope that perhaps even he might be made whole.

1. Because of the unique acoustics of the hills, the man with leprosy could hear every word that Jesus was speaking, and every word He spoke carried an immeasurable depth of understanding and empathy for the man's everyday fears. What words of compassion from Jesus did this man hear (see Matt. 6:28–30)? What was the effect of these words on him?

2. After all the years of being rejected and living as an outcast, what did Jesus' words mean to him such that they filled his heart with wonder?

3. What did hearing the words of Jesus cause the man with leprosy to do?

4. What was Jesus doing as the man with leprosy decided to seek Him out and began to make his way toward Jesus?

5. Overwhelmed, the man with leprosy fell at Jesus' feet, worshiped Him with tears, and whispered, "Lord, if You are willing, You can make me clean." What was Jesus' immediate response and its results?

Hiding didn't get the man with leprosy in Matthew 8 the healing and restoration he needed. Fortunately, hearing about the goodness of God—how God wanted to be a loving Father to him and take care of all his needs—got him out of hiding and into seeking the Lord for his miracle. It changed his mind from seeing a God Who ostracized and condemned unclean people to seeing a God Who loved them no matter what their condition. This change of mind lit his faith and put courage in his heart to seek and receive the healing he so desperately wanted.

Like the man with leprosy, could you also be hiding from God today? Maybe you've been struggling with an addiction or cycle of defeat, had a failed marriage or business, or made some bad decisions. And maybe your failure has caused you to avoid God, avoid going to church, and avoid people in general. Beloved, whatever may be causing you to feel "unclean" or disqualified today, God wants you to change your mind about Him and, instead of hiding from Him, to run to Him!

6. **According to Romans 10:17, how does faith for your miracle come?**

7. **Why is what you hear about God of utmost importance?**

8. **What does Acts 10:38 tell us about what God wants to do for you?**

9. **If Jesus is God's will in action, and He went about doing good in the Gospels, what does this tell you about what God is really like?**

If you want to have faith for your breakthrough, make sure you are hearing and believing right about God through "the word of Christ," which refers to the word of the *new covenant*, the word of *His grace*.

In the book of Acts, the apostle Paul says, "So now, brethren, I commend you to God and to the word of His grace, which is able to build you up and give you an inheritance among all those who are sanctified" (Acts 20:32). What is able to build you up and give you an inheritance among the saints? It is the word of His grace or the word of Christ. The Bible exhorts us to "Let the word of Christ dwell in you richly in all wisdom" (Col. 3:16).

10. So if you're feeling discouraged or fearful, or if the prognosis you've heard isn't good, what should your first priority be?

When you have the word of Christ dwelling richly in you, His love and grace will cause you to overcome every temptation and fear, slay your giants, and live life with greater boldness and victory!

Calli's heartrending story (page 40) profoundly demonstrates how the word of Christ has the power to change your life.

11. What had Calli been taught that led to constant fear?

If you've also entertained fears about God, how has your view of God been changing as you're going through this guide?

12. How did the response of other Christians toward her ultimately affect her? Conversely, what was the Lord's response toward her?

All of Calli's chains of darkness, insanity, and addictions were broken when she heard about Jesus and His grace and how Jesus said nothing could take us out of His hands. The Lord spoke to her heart and said, "My child, I have held you in the palm of My hands all these years that you have stumbled, fallen, and wandered. I have called you, and waited for you to turn and hear My voice. You are Mine."

13. As you reread Calli's encounter with Jesus, take a moment to bring your specific situation to your loving Savior, Jesus, and write down His words of comfort and grace to you.

Have you ever wondered what gives a person the strength to become a champion, such as Daniel or David in the Scriptures? Read pages 43–44 and consider the amazing things they did and the persons they became.

14. **What does Daniel 11:32 tell us about becoming a champion?**

15. **Do you desire to be like Daniel—to walk in strength, wisdom, and favor that is undeniable and irresistible, to see miracles and breakthroughs in your life? What is the key?**

16. **David challenged and took down Goliath when others were cowering in fear, and David became a man after God's own heart. What did David know that you need to know, as it will help you grow today?**

God's love has to be experienced in your heart. Head knowledge—just knowing intellectually that God loves you because He loves everyone—isn't going to cut it. It is when you really encounter the person of Jesus and His grace, and really know in your heart that He loves *you*, that positive and profound changes begin to happen in your life.

17. Second Peter 1:2 says, "Grace and peace be multiplied to you in the knowledge of God and of Jesus our Lord." What does the meaning of the Greek word for "knowledge" (see page 46) tell us about the power of hearing about the Lord Jesus and His love?

18. Having read Gideon's story on page 44, perhaps you feel like he did, small and powerless in the face of your challenges. What gracious, encouraging words did Gideon hear and embrace that you can as well to find strength and wisdom and fulfill your destiny?

CHAPTER 4

RECEIVE THE GREATEST BLESSING

The key to living with greater confidence and boldness is knowing, first and foremost, that all your sins are forgiven. Today, as a beloved child of God, know that your heavenly Father is not mad at you. All yours sins have been judged and punished in the body of Jesus at the cross.

There are many believers battling guilt, fear, and condemnation because they are not confident that *all* their sins have been forgiven once and for all. They inadvertently hide from their heavenly Father when they fail, like Adam and Eve hid in the Garden of Eden, instead of coming boldly to His throne of grace to obtain mercy and find grace to help them when they need it the most (see Heb. 4:16 NLT).

1. **In Joni's heartwarming testimony (page 48), how had she viewed God?**

2. **As Joni began to read about the grace of God, what discovery did she make that transformed not only her life but her relationships with her children, parents, and even with herself?**

3. **Joni's life began to turn around when she received the revelation that all her sins, mistakes, and bad decisions are forgiven. Do you have this assurance that all your sins have been forgiven?**

The moment you invited Jesus into your heart as your Lord and Savior, all your sins were forgiven—your past sins, your present sins, and your future sins. The Word of God tells us, "In Him we have redemption through His blood, the forgiveness of sins, according to the riches of His grace" (Eph. 1:7). Once you are born again, you are in Christ. You do not have to try to get forgiveness. You *have* the forgiveness of sins, and this forgiveness of sins that you have is not according to what you have done, but according to the riches of God's grace—His unmerited, unearned, and undeserved favor!

4. **The good news of the gospel is that our Lord and Savior, Jesus Christ, sacrificed Himself at the cross and His perfect, sinless blood provided forgiveness for all our sins. How did David describe the blessedness of a man whose sins are forgiven in Roman 4:7–8 (NLT)?**

5. **Conversely, when believers start to question if they are truly forgiven, what does it lead to?**

Meditate on Romans 4:7–8 and on the blessing of God's forgiveness, so dearly paid for and so freely given to us. Let this truth anchor and put strength in your heart, and drive away every fear and sense of insecurity.

Colossians 1:13–14 tells believers who have been born again in Christ that God the Father "has delivered us from the power of darkness and conveyed us into the kingdom of the Son of His love, in whom we have redemption through His blood, the forgiveness of sins." Notice the *change of location*. You used to be under the power of darkness. But the moment you believed in Jesus, you were moved and placed under the blood of Jesus, where there is perpetual forgiveness of sins.

To understand the total forgiveness of sins, we have to understand the value of the one Man, Jesus, Who sacrificed Himself on the cross for us. He alone, because He was sinless, could pay for all the sins of every man when He died at Calvary. He took the judgment, punishment, and condemnation for all humanity's sins upon Himself.

6. **Read Romans 10:9–13 carefully. While everyone's sin is paid for, does that mean that everyone is automatically forgiven? How does Scripture state that a person becomes a born-again believer in Christ?**

To be saved, every individual needs to make a personal decision to receive the forgiveness of all their sins by receiving Jesus as their personal Lord and Savior. The teaching that everyone will ultimately be saved without receiving Jesus and His finished work at the cross is heresy.

7. **First Corinthians 15:17, 20–22 tells us there is no assurance that all our sins have been forgiven without the resurrection of Jesus. What else does it tell us that gives you assurance of your forgiveness in Christ?**

Our forgiveness is not contingent upon us and what we have or have not done, so no one can boast that they earned their forgiveness through their own efforts. "For by grace you have been saved through faith, and that not of yourselves; it is the gift of God, not of works, lest anyone should boast" (Eph. 2:8–9). Through faith in Jesus' finished work at the cross, we have received the gift of salvation. When something is a gift, it means that you cannot work for it, earn it, or merit it. A gift is lavished upon the recipient by the giver, and Jesus gave of His own life to ransom yours.

8. **Reread Ephesians 2:8–9. How are you saved? How have all your sins been forgiven? How have you been made righteous?**

This is your unshakable foundation built upon the finished work of Jesus Christ. Don't allow any teaching to diminish the cross of Jesus in your life and make salvation, forgiveness, and righteousness blessings you have to work at in order to maintain and keep.

9. **Righteousness is not about right doing. Righteousness is about right believing. According to Romans 5:18–19, how are you made righteous?**

10. **When you are buffeted by voices of accusation and condemnation over your failures, what do you need to believe and declare to see God's favor and every benefit of His finished work released into your situation?**

There are people who teach that when we receive Jesus, all our past sins are forgiven, but our future sins are only forgiven as we confess them and ask God for forgiveness. Let's look at what the Scriptures declare.

11. Ephesians 1:7 states "In Him we *have* redemption through His blood, the forgiveness of sins, according to the riches of His grace" (emphasis mine). What does the original Greek verb for "have" indicate?

12. Furthermore, in 1 John 2:12, it says, "I write to you, little children, because your sins are forgiven you for His name's sake." What do we learn from the Greek tense used here for "are forgiven"?

13. Colossian 2:13–14 (NLT) states that when we were dead because of our sins, "God made you alive with Christ, for he forgave *all* our sins. He canceled the record of the charges against us and took it away by nailing it to the cross" (emphasis mine). What does the word "all" mean in the Greek, and what does that mean to you as a believer?

Hebrews 10:14 says, "For by one offering He [Jesus] has perfected forever those who are being sanctified." How long are you perfected? *Forever!* How can you be perfected forever, if your future sins are not forgiven? Obviously, they are!

Many believers are worried that people will take advantage of the revelation of their total forgiveness in Christ and go on to lead godless lives. They are worried that such teaching places no emphasis on sanctification or the desire to live holy, God-glorifying lives. Because this is so crucial to understand, please study pages 58–60 closely.

Hebrews 10:14 says that we are *being sanctified* even though we are *perfected forever* by Christ's one act of obedience at the cross. That means that the moment you received Jesus, you were instantaneously forgiven, cleansed of all sin, justified by faith, and made perfectly righteousness by the blood of Jesus. As a believer, you cannot become more righteous, but you can become more holy in how you live.

14. What does *sanctification* mean? How do you become more holy?

Sanctification or the desire to live holy lives is all about grace. Contrary to what many people imagine, the revelation of forgiveness does not detract from, nor is it at the expense of, right living. Instead, *grace is the fuel that makes right living happen.*

15. What do 2 Timothy 2:1 and 2 Peter 3:18 tell you about establishing yourself in the gospel of grace?

A precious brother wrote and provided a beautiful, true-life picture of what really happens when a person receives the revelation of his forgiveness in Christ. He wrote, "Previously, when I was *trying* to be a good Christian, I was only *crawling* along, inch by inch. But now that I've got hold of grace, I'm *running* in my relationship with God! The more I learn about God's amazing grace, the more I desperately want to glorify Him with my life!" The gospel of grace brought him into an intimacy with God that he had previously only dreamed about.

Grace produces true holiness. The more you grow in grace—the more you are washed, again and again, by the water of the word of God's grace—the more you grow in sanctification and holiness, and the more you allow the Holy Spirit to correct habits and thinking that keep you in bondage. Beloved, when you experience the grace of our Lord Jesus, the allure and passing pleasures of sin fade in the light of His glory and grace. Victory also begins to come into previous areas of struggle, weakness, and defeat.

16. **Grace will set you free to have the kind of relationship you always longed for with God, one that is intimate, powerful, and full of peace, joy, and good fruit. Take a moment to come to your loving Savior and receive His grace and the assurance of His total forgiveness of your sins. Write a simple prayer, thanking Him for how much you have been forgiven.**

CHAPTER 5

BEGIN LIVING WITH CONFIDENCE

When you understand the power of Jesus' ever-cleansing blood, it changes your life forever. Fear and depression give way to indescribable peace and joy. No longer do you feel insecure in your salvation because you possess the blessed assurance that Christ's eternal and efficacious blood has cleansed you and continues to cleanse you of every sin!

Frances Ridley Havergal, a famous English hymn writer of the nineteenth century, battled with fear, insecurity, and depression. Despite being extremely gifted and receiving Christ as her Savior at a young age and loving the Lord deeply, she was convinced her "great wickedness of heart" impeded a full and intimate walk with the Lord.

1. **What did Frances long for in her relationship with God?**

2. **First John 1:7 says, "But if we walk in the light as He is in the light, we have fellowship with one another, and the blood of Jesus Christ His Son cleanses us from all sin." What revelation did Frances receive about the Greek word for "cleanses" that lifted her out of her depths of despair?**

"As we may trust [Jesus] to cleanse us from the stain of past sins so we may trust Him to cleanse us from all present defilement; yes, *all*!"

Frances Havergal's powerful revelation of the ever-cleansing blood of Jesus opened the door of "a very glory of hope and joy" to her heart. Following that revelation she wrote one of her well-loved hymns, *Like a River Glorious*. Read the lyrics of this beautiful hymn on pages 67–68.

3. **How was Frances' life transformed from the inside-out as yours can also be?**

4. **Because Jesus' blood continually cleanses you, you cannot bounce in and out of the light of Christ, in and out of being forgiven, justified, and made righteous, and in and out of fellowship with God. What assurance does this give you about your salvation in Christ?**

Many believers are taught that Hebrews 10:26–29 warns us that if we sin willfully, we can lose our salvation and expect God's "judgment, and fiery indignation." As a result, these believers become sin-conscious—always mindful and worried that they might have sinned willfully and that God's judgment would come on them. When something bad happens to them (they contract a disease, for example), they immediately attribute it to God's judgment of their mistakes. Having this fear and perpetual judgment-consciousness is not how God the Father wants us to live.

Almost every sin we commit after being saved (the exceptions being sins we commit unconsciously) is committed willfully. So this can't be what Hebrews 10:26 is talking about, or every believer would be living each day expecting God's judgment! What does it mean, then, to "sin willfully"? Is it something that a believer can do?

Pages 72–77 provide a detailed study of this Scripture. Read it again and consider it in its context so you can resolve this once and for all.

5. **To whom was the book of Hebrews written, and to whom, in particular, was Hebrews 10:26–29 written?**

6. **In this context, to "sin willfully" is to commit what specific sin?**

7. So why is it that Hebrews 10:26–29 cannot be addressing believers and is not referring to Christians who are "backsliding" or "going astray" or Christians who sin in a moment of weakness or temptation?

8. The Greek word for "judgment" in Hebrews 10:27 is *krisis,* which means a sentence of "condemnation and punishment." To whom does this really apply?

9. So what did Jesus say in John 5:24 when it comes to judgment and *God's children*? Should believers ever fear the Lord's judgment?

Know this in your heart: as believers of Jesus, all of us have believed to the saving of our souls for all eternity. True believers need never fear the Lord's judgment, as all the fire of judgment fell fully on our Lord Jesus as He carried our sins at Calvary. Hallelujah!

First John 1:9 states, "If we confess our sins, He is faithful and just to forgive us our sins and to cleanse us from all unrighteousness." Many believers say this verse teaches that believers must keep confessing their sins in order to be forgiven and cleansed of all unrighteousness. Please study pages 78–84 for an analysis of the context and application of this verse.

10. If in order to be "right with God" we must confess *every* sin, what problems does this pose?

In the two instances where we see the word "sins" in 1 John 1:9, it is the Greek noun *hamartia* that is used. *Hamartia* ("a missing of the mark") indicates "a principle or source of action, or an inward element producing acts . . . a governing principle or power." It refers to the sin principle, or our sinful state on account of Adam's sin. By using the noun form of this word, John was clearly not referring to our committing of individual acts of sin, or he would have used the verb form, *hamartano*.

11. In the light of this, what confession of sins does John mean here?

First John 1:9 is primarily a salvation verse, one that encourages the sinner to acknowledge and confess his sinful state or "sinnerhood," get born again by faith in our Lord Jesus Christ, and have his sinful state through Adam replaced with a new righteous state through Christ.

12. How often do we need to do this?

Just two verses later, John states: "My little children, these things I write to you, so that you may not sin. And if anyone sins, we have an Advocate with the Father, Jesus Christ the righteous" (1 John 2:1). This time, the words "sin" and "sins" are the Greek verb *hamartano*. Here, John is referring to believers' committing of sins—their sinful thoughts and deeds.

13. What is John reminding believers about when they fail?

The Bible's answer to overcoming sin is always to remind believers of their righteous identity in Christ. This is not to encourage us to sin but to encourage us to look to our Lord Jesus, to see our sins punished at the cross and to live victoriously and gloriously for Him. Remember that true repentance is all about turning to the cross and returning to His grace!

14. As believers, do we confess our sins *to be* forgiven?

15. How does knowing this help us be honest with God about our shortcomings and receive His grace to overcome them?

The cleansing power of Jesus' shed blood is the launching pad to living life with greater boldness and confidence. Boldness comes when you realize that because of Jesus' cleansing blood, you don't need to hide from God, afraid that He is out to get you for your sins. You can have boldness to enter the holiest presence of God with a heart that fully trusts Him, and with a conscience that is free of guilt and condemnation. This is the new and life-giving way God wants you to live by, one where you can confidently approach His throne of grace at any time to receive His mercy, favor, help, blessings, and life!

16. Take a moment to thank the Father for the ever-efficacious blood of Jesus that gives you the assurance you can always come boldly to His throne of grace to receive strength, help, and wisdom from Him. If there is an area of struggle that is troubling you or keeping you in defeat, talk to Him now, knowing that you don't have to hide from Him nor be afraid that He is out to get you for it.

KEY 2

BUILD A FOUNDATION FOR LASTING BREAKTHROUGHS

CHAPTER 6

WHY PREACH GRACE?

The *Grace Revolution* was written to help you build a strong foundation for lasting breakthroughs. Whatever defeat you may be struggling with now, anchor yourself in God's grace by receiving and understanding the gospel of grace from His Word. Don't base your understanding of God's heart toward you on hearsay or man's opinion. Base it on the unshakable and eternal foundation of His Word.

1. **According to Luke 4:18–19, what did our Lord Jesus proclaim would be the results of the preaching of the true gospel?**

Here is a foundational Scripture to get deep inside your heart: "For the law was given through Moses, but grace and truth came through Jesus Christ" (John 1:17). The law that was given through Moses refers to the Sinaitic covenant that was made between God and Israel. Our covenant is the new covenant of grace and truth that *came* through God's own Son, Jesus Christ, at the cross.

2. **What do you need to realize about "grace and truth" as contrasted to the law?**

3. **Why is knowing this distinction between the law and grace so important?**

4. **When Jesus said to the woman who was caught in adultery, "Neither do I condemn you; go and sin no more" (John 8:11), how does that show grace and truth working together as a composite whole?**

Romans 6:14 says "sin shall not have dominion over you," yet many sincere believers still end up trapped in a cycle of sin, defeat, and condemnation. Pages 94–95 include a practical illustration of how indulgences quickly develop into an addiction that imprisons a person in guilt and self-condemnation, which only perpetuates the problem. The Cycle of Defeat diagram helps show you how those who are under constant guilt and condemnation have no strength to overcome temptation and end up repeating their sins and living a painful life trapped in a cycle of defeat.

Now look at the Cycle of Victory diagram on page 98 and consider how righteousness-consciousness ultimately propels a believer in that same position to increasingly live a life above defeat.

5. **Perhaps you can relate to a believer going through the cycle of defeat. What are you learning about how to get off this cycle and get on the cycle of victory?**

6. What is the first step we should take to go from a place where like the apostle Paul we lament, "I want to do what is good, but I don't. I don't want to do what is wrong, but I do it anyway. . . . Oh, what a miserable person I am!" (Rom. 7:19, 24 NLT), to a place of lasting victory?

So when the next temptation comes, right in the midst of that temptation, believe and say this from your heart as did the apostle Paul: "Therefore there is now no condemnation for those who are in Christ Jesus" (Rom. 8:1 NASB). Instead of believing that you are a failure of a Christian and that God is angry with you, begin to believe and declare boldly, "I *am* the righteousness of God in Christ Jesus! Because I am in Christ Jesus, there is therefore now *no* condemnation for me! Fellowship with my heavenly Father is *not* broken and I am *still* His beloved child—highly favored and deeply loved by Him—all because of Jesus' finished work!"

7. Why is believing and declaring that you are righteous so important?

Whatever your struggle today, it is this revelation of your forgiveness, righteousness, and no condemnation in Christ that will set you free. This is what happened to Neil (page 98) who was liberated from a forty-year struggle with a sexual addiction and a life of fear, guilt, and condemnation.

8. **What revelation did Neil receive that broke this addiction off his life?**

9. **What does Neil do when he is tempted to sin again?**

Second Corinthians 5:17–21 (NLT) states: ". . . anyone who belongs to Christ has become a new person. The old life is gone; a new life has begun! And all of this is a gift from God, who brought us back to himself through Christ. . . . For God made Christ, who never sinned, to be the offering for our sin, so that we could be made right with God through Christ."

10. **As a believer, have you actively received the gift of righteousness that you have in Christ? How is the revelation of your forgiveness, being made right with God, and no condemnation in Christ making a difference in your life?**

11. The apostle Paul tells us in Romans 1:16 that the gospel of grace releases "the power of God" to bring His salvation into your life. Does the word "salvation" just mean being saved from hell to go to heaven?

12. Romans 1:17 says, "For in [the gospel] the righteousness of God is revealed from faith to faith; as it is written, 'The just shall live by faith.'" According to this verse, what is it that makes the gospel of grace so powerful?

13. "The just [or righteous] shall live by faith." Now that you know you have God's gifts of no condemnation and righteousness in Christ, how will this change the way you respond to condemnation and discouragement that come when you have failed?

As you practice righteousness-consciousness, journal how your new responses are leading you to a life of increasing victory.

CHAPTER 7

WILL THE REAL GOSPEL PLEASE STAND UP?

A life that is founded upon the gospel of Jesus Christ is unshakable. When you build your life upon the gospel, you are building on a strong foundation that will give you stability and the power of God for lasting breakthroughs (see Rom. 1:16).

You may be going through an extremely difficult season right now. Perhaps you need a healing, provision, employment, or relationship breakthrough. Invite our Lord Jesus into your situation. Involve Him in your area of need. See and believe that the Lord is with you and for you.

1. **What does Proverbs 18:10 tell us to do for whatever our need is?**

Learn to speak this promise of God over your situations: " 'No weapon formed against you shall prosper, and every tongue which rises against you in judgment you shall condemn. This is the heritage of the servants of the LORD, and their righteousness is from Me,' says the LORD" (Isa. 54:17).

2. **Meditate on the last sentence of this powerful Scripture. What does this say about your righteousness in Christ? What will a revelation of this bring for you?**

3. **Believers who are not established in their righteous identity in Christ are susceptible to the weapons of the enemy, such as sickness, lack, guilt, and fear. Why is it so important you are listening to the real gospel?**

The Old Testament account of the exodus from Egypt provides many illustrations that confirm the truth that only grace, found in the person of Jesus Christ, can lead us into the promised land.

4. **Moses, who represents the law, is dead (see Josh. 1:2). And only Joshua (*Yehowshua* in Hebrew), a type of Christ, can bring us into the promised land. What does that tell us about how we inherit God's promises today?**

5. **God's people did not use their own might to push down the walls of Jericho. The walls crumbled at the blast of the rams' horns and with a great shout from the people. What is the ram's horn a picture of?**

6. **What the ten plagues of Moses could not do, the lambs' blood applied to the lintels and doorposts of the Hebrew homes caused Pharaoh (a type of Satan) to finally release God's people from captivity. What does the lambs' blood typify?**

Only the love and grace of our Lord Jesus, Who shed His blood at Calvary for you, can set you free and deliver you from every bondage. The true gospel, that shows you how you are justified by your faith in Christ's sacrifice at the cross, not by your own works, empowers you to break free and reign in life. It makes bondages and addictions crumble and fall away like the walls of Jericho did!

The apostle Jude tells us to "contend earnestly for the faith which was once for all delivered to the saints" (Jude 1:3). When you hear the word "faith" mentioned in the New Testament, it refers to "justification by faith"—how one is made righteous before God based solely on his faith in Christ Jesus. *This is the crux of the gospel of Jesus Christ.* This is why the gospel is called "good news" and this is what sets it apart from all false gospels. This is the gospel we are to *contend earnestly* for, which means "to agonize for." We are to fight for the truth that we are justified by faith and not works.

7. **Unfortunately, what message are many believers hearing that subtly replaces the good news of justification by faith with justification by works?**

Is that message familiar to you? What has been your response to it?

Right living is certainly important, but the crux of the gospel is justification by faith, not right living or good works. Right living comes by believing right in the gospel.

8. If you still find yourself living by faith in your works to please God, how can you move to the place of living from faith to *faith*, believing at every point you are saved and justified by Christ alone? Which do you think results in greater intimacy with God and in victory?

9. In Sally's testimony on page 113, she describes her life as being held in the agonizing grip of condemnation after listening to teaching that contained a mixture of condemnation and grace. What powerful word set her free?

10. How has Sally's life changed dramatically since she discovered and believed that she has been justified by the blood of Christ?

In Romans 10:2–3 (NLT), Paul warns about a misguided zeal, which was prevalent among his Jewish brethren: "I know what enthusiasm they have for God, but it is misdirected zeal. For they don't understand God's way of making people right with himself. Refusing to accept God's way, they cling to their own way of getting right with God by trying to keep the law."

11. What is the irony of believers trying to keep God's laws to be righteous?

12. Before Paul lists the fruit of the Spirit in Galatians 5, what truth did he take them back to in the previous chapters?

13. Galatians 5:22–23 lists the fruit of the Spirit as "love, joy, peace, longsuffering, kindness, goodness, faithfulness, gentleness, self-control." How does true holiness/right living, as defined by the fruit of the Spirit, come?

CHAPTER 8

FREEDOM FROM SELF-CONDEMNATION

Cruel words spoken in anger. A betrayal of trust. Promises broken. A destructive relationship you knew you should not have entered into.

Have you been down those dark paths before? There are so many people who are living in the shadow of guilt and condemnation. Mistakes of the past haunt them and it is a painfully lonely and arduous journey for them.

1. Perhaps the paralyzed man who was carried to Jesus and let down through the roof by his four faithful friends understood a little of this. When Jesus saw their faith, He said to the paralytic, "Son, your sins are forgiven you" (Mark 2:5). What the man clearly needed was healing, so what did forgiveness have to do with his condition or healing, and what was the result?

2. If you are paralyzed by a heavy sense of condemnation over something in your past, what hope and assurance does this story bring?

Your brightest and most glorious days are still ahead of you.

Even though you may not be able to see right now the good things that God has for your future, Scripture says, "God has revealed them to us through His Spirit. . . . Now we have received, not the spirit of the world, but the Spirit who is from God, that we might know the things that have been freely given to us by God" (1 Cor. 2:10, 12).

3. **What are these precious and priceless gifts that God has freely given to us?**

4. **Amazingly, the Holy Spirit now lives *in* us and abides with us *forever*. What took place in our lives that allows this to be true?**

5. **Ephesians 1:13–14 also says that when we believed in Jesus, we "were sealed with the Holy Spirit of promise." What does that mean?**

6. **The praise report from Pete on page 125 reflects how when you hear the pure gospel preached, the Holy Spirit in you responds with great joy and great peace. What did Pete feel like and what has been its fruit?**

It is so vital that you believe in God's love for you. Because of His superabundant grace, your past doesn't have to determine your future. In Christ, you have a new life, a new beginning, and a new future.

Read the precious testimony from Daphne, a recovered alcoholic, on pages 125–127 and see this truth reflected. After being saved for five years, she was still full of self-condemnation and thought Jesus was very angry with her and that she needed to try to be good.

7. **What does Daphne say makes self-condemnation and this misbelief about God so devastating to alcoholics (and similarly to everyone else)?**

8. **What did Daphne hear and believe that brought healing into her life?**

Condemnation kills! It is a dangerous and vicious trap that keeps you imprisoned. It eats at you from the inside out, and you can't just will it away or tell yourself to forget about the mistakes and bad choices you have made. Our sins demand a resolution. The wages of sin is death (see Rom. 6:23). Our conscience cries out against us and demands that punishment for our sins be meted out.

9. **What is the *only* answer that will satisfy the guilty conscience?**

True freedom is only possible with right believing about what the divine exchange at the cross of Calvary has accomplished for you.

Understanding the power of the finished work of Jesus on the cross and how you are totally justified by faith is the only foundation for lasting breakthroughs and genuine inside-out transformation. You can evaluate how well you understand what Jesus accomplished at the cross for you by looking at how free you are in Christ today. Are you constantly struggling with thoughts of fear, doubt, guilt, and condemnation? Are you persistently entangled in a sinful habit or addiction?

10. **What produces real victory over sin and lasting breakthroughs from fears, addictions, and bondages?**

11. **What is the connection between being strong in the gospel of grace and living a godly, holy, and glorious life?**

12. **True grace produces the power to sin no more but it doesn't stop there. It also produces good works. How is that seen in Daphne's life?**

James 2:24 says, "You see then that a man is justified by works, and not by faith only." Some believers read this and fall back into trying to be justified by works. What they don't realize is that what James is referring to is *justification before men* (i.e. other people), not our justification before God. Jesus said, "Let your light so shine *before men*, that they may see your good works and glorify your Father in heaven" (Matt. 5:16, emphasis mine). Who sees your good works? Men. James said, "If a brother or sister is naked and destitute of daily food, and one of you says to them, 'Depart in peace, be warmed and filled,' but you do not give them the things which are needed for the body, what does it profit? Thus also faith by itself, if it does not have works, is dead" (James 2:15–17). Notice how the good work of giving to the needy is done before men and to men?

13. In what way do our works justify us before other people?

14. Many churches put so much pressure on new believers to produce good works immediately, and when these new believers don't meet the expectations, they end up in self-condemnation. Why is patience with new believers important?

15. What do you need to know and what should you do when you've made mistakes and bad decisions and feel discouraged by your failures or feel that God is disappointed with you?

CHAPTER 9

EXPERIENCE FREEDOM FROM FEAR

Fear is a destructive bondage. Fear paralyzes you and prevents you from fulfilling the amazing destiny that God has for you. Fear makes you feel inadequate and insecure, and comes with unhealthy side effects ranging from panic attacks to sleep disorders. Fear is irrational. Fear is a spiritual condition, which is why you can't reason fear away. You can't simply tell someone who is struggling with fear and gripped by panic attacks to just stop being fearful. A spiritual condition cannot be remedied naturally. Fear can be eradicated only by a personal encounter with the person of Jesus.

If fear is all too familiar to you, know that it is not your heavenly Father's heart for you to live tormented by fear.

1. **What amazing promise is given in 1 John 4:18?**

2. **John 3:16 tells us, "For God *so loved* the world that He gave His only begotten Son, that whoever believes in Him should not perish but have everlasting life." Take a moment to meditate on this verse. What do the two words "so loved" tell you about the intensity of God's love for you? How did He demonstrate this love for you? How does this make you feel?**

How we see God is important, because a faulty perception of God can cause sincere people to have an unhealthy, lifetime fear of God. Many people have a wrong impression of God, because for generations people have portrayed Him as hard, angry, unfeeling, and condemning, just waiting for man to trip up. When they believe that God is against them and out to punish them, they live in fear of Him, and find it impossible to break out of their sins, addictions, anxieties, and fears.

3. **How has God been portrayed to you? What impact has your perception of God had upon your life?**

Scripture reveals to you God's true nature. First John 4:8 states, "God is love." Psalm 86:15 (NIV) says, "But you, Lord, are a compassionate and gracious God, slow to anger, abounding in love and faithfulness." Daniel 9:9 (NIV) states, "The Lord our God is merciful and forgiving." Psalm 25:6 says, "O LORD, Your tender mercies and Your lovingkindnesses . . . they are from of old."

4. **This is our God according to the Holy Word! List His attributes and take a moment to thank Him that He is, always and unchangingly, all these things toward you.**

To further understand the true nature of God, just look at Jesus. He said, "He who has seen Me has seen the Father. . . . The words that I speak to you I do not speak on My own authority; but the Father who dwells in Me does the works" (John 14:9–10).

5. **How did Jesus speak to and treat sinners and the outcasts of society in the Gospels? What about those who were self-righteous and resisted His grace?**

6. **The haters of Jesus labeled Him "a friend of sinners" to cast aspersions on His integrity (see Matt. 11:19). How is this derogatory label really a beautiful picture of His grace?**

Sinners found hope, joy, and liberty in Jesus. He never condoned their sins, but He also never rejected them. He showed them His grace and His grace transformed them from living a life of sin to living a life of holiness.

7. **How does Jesus' befriending the corrupt tax collector, Zacchaeus, demonstrate both His love for sinners as well as the power of grace to change a person's life from the inside out?**

Grace produces true holiness.

Zacchaeus was transformed by grace. Justification by faith produces hope, peace, and joy and a heart for Jesus that results in good fruit. In contrast, the rich young ruler, who came to Jesus saying, "Good Teacher, what shall I do to inherit eternal life?" wanted to be justified by his works (Luke 18:18).

8. **This rich young ruler believed that he could, and that he had kept God's laws. Why did Jesus give him more of the law, and what did it result in?**

9. **The law *demands*, grace *supplies*. When you come under the law and become demand-conscious, what is often the result? Conversely, when you come under grace and believe God will work in you and for you in every challenge, how different are the results?**

10. **Unfortunately, like the rich young ruler, there are many believers who after they have been saved are taught and believe that they can be justified before God only by their works. Because no man can meet the demands of the law and be justified, fear is inadvertently the result. How does fear rob them of the joy of living?**

   If that also describes you, how has what you've learned in this chapter changed your thinking about condemnation and punishment from God?

Listen to your Father's heartbeat in Jesus' words: "For God did not send His Son into the world to condemn the world, but that the world through Him might be saved. He who believes in Him is not condemned" (John 3: 17–18).

See how the apostle Paul describes the Ten Commandments in 2 Corinthians 3:7–9: "But if the ministry of death, written and engraved on stones, was glorious . . . how will the ministry of the Spirit not be more glorious? For if the ministry of condemnation had glory, the ministry of righteousness exceeds much more in glory."

11. **How do the Ten Commandments minister death and create fear in a believer who chooses to live under the Mosaic law? In contrast, what does the covenant of grace minister, thereby setting a believer free from fear?**

12. **Let us be clear: the Ten Commandments are glorious! The problem has always been imperfect man's ability to keep God's perfect law. At the cross, what did our Lord Jesus do on our behalf to deal with the demands of the law on us (see Matt. 5:17)? Why did He do this?**

13. **We are in the age of God's glorious grace. How are you liberated when you realize God sees you righteous by faith in Christ and not by your works?**

Through the sacrifice of God's Son and the perfection of Christ's finished work, He has made a way for you to live free from the captivity of fear.

No discussion of fear would be complete without a focus on the mother of all fears, which is the fear of death. Hebrews 2:14–15 gives this in detail: "Inasmuch then as the children have partaken of flesh and blood, He Himself likewise shared in the same, that through death He might destroy him who had the power of death, that is, the devil, and release those who through fear of death were all their lifetime subject to bondage."

14. **Despite God's clear promise of release, why do believers still come under the fear of death?**

    Is this a struggle you are familiar with? How can you actively receive God's grace in this area?

15. **What is the good news that Hebrews 2:14–15 declares?**

You can know beyond the shadow of any doubt that Jesus, through His death at the cross, has set you free from the fear of death, and with it every bondage you may be in right now.

16. In Ursula's testimony on pages 153–154, how does she describe how she found freedom from all her fears, including her debilitating fear of death?

Because you are a believer in Jesus, God's Word victoriously proclaims that "Christ purchased our freedom [redeeming us] from the curse (doom) of the Law [and its condemnation] by [Himself] becoming a curse for us, for it is written [in the Scriptures], Cursed is everyone who hangs on a tree (is crucified)" (Gal. 3:13 AMP). You have been redeemed!

17. Take some time to go back over this chapter and meditate on how the liberating truths from the Word of God apply to you personally. What has the Lord been speaking to your heart about His perfect love for you and the intimate relationship He desires to have with you?

CHAPTER 10

GLORIOUS GRACE

The Word of God tells us, "Awake to righteousness, and sin not" (1 Cor. 15:34 KJV). The grace revolution is a great awakening to righteousness. When people hear the real gospel that tells them how right Jesus' finished work has made them, they begin to grasp just how loved, valued, and precious they are in Christ. From then on, they begin to realize that they don't have to live in defeat, live bound to addictions, and live in fear or failure. Instead of seeing someone worthless when they look in the mirror, they see a highly favored, greatly blessed, and deeply loved child of the Most High God!

1. **In Kirk's testimony (pages 157–159), he shared how the more he tried to do right, the more he failed, and because of his weaknesses and failures, he believed he would never escape God's curses and hellfire. Despite attending church and Bible study regularly, he was tormented by fear and wondered if he would make it to heaven. What did he hear that led to his turnaround and restoration?**

2. **What happened when Kirk surrendered completely to the power of God's grace and said yes to Jesus?**

3. **From once being beaten down by shortcomings, hopelessness, and addictions, what helps Kirk walk with boldness today?**

"Awake to righteousness" and realize just how unconditionally and irrevocably loved you are by God.

Even as God restores the glorious truth of the gospel of grace to the body of Christ, the enemy also produces a counterfeit grace to try to confuse people and make them wary of true grace. But don't be discouraged or afraid that you might be misled by counterfeit grace. Just be skillful in God's Word and learn how to discern what is scriptural by reading God's Word for yourself. Build a strong foundation on the true gospel of grace.

4. **What is the simplest way to know if what you are hearing is the gospel of grace?**

5. **Why is the teaching called "universal reconciliation," which claims *everyone* will ultimately be saved, a heresy?**

6. **There are also "teachers" who propagate the error that since believers are under grace, they do not come under God's correction. That is absolutely a lie. Under the new covenant of grace, how does God correct His children, and why is it so vital to be a part of a local church with good leaders?**

Under the new covenant of grace, God does *not* correct His children by using accidents, premature deaths, sicknesses, and diseases.

7. The apostle Paul corrected those in the Corinthian church who got entangled in sin and sexual immorality by asking them, "Do you not know that your bodies are members of Christ?" (see 1 Cor. 6:15–20). What is he reminding them of?

We receive God's correction by being reminded of our righteous identity in Christ, which gives us the power to overcome sin and reign in every area through the abundance of grace and the gift of righteousness. We have been purchased with a price, a heavy price at the cross, and are now called to live for the glory of our Lord Jesus. *Grace* is the power to go and sin no more (see John 8:11)!

8. According to 1 John 4:19, where does the power to love and live a holy life come from?

Holiness is a fruit of God's grace. First experience and taste the grace of God and His love will surely cause you to live a holy life!

Christianity is all about God's love for you. It is His love for and in you that results in inward heart transformation. Christianity is not a religion; it is a relationship. Christianity is not about a list of dos and don'ts; it is about intimacy, love, and a warm, beating heart.

9. **God's Word says that "you are in Christ Jesus, who has become for us wisdom from God—that is, our righteousness, holiness and redemption" (1 Cor. 1:30 NIV). Jesus Himself is your wisdom, your righteousness, and also your holiness! Because our holiness or sanctification is found in the person of Jesus, what should we do when we are tempted to sin?**

10. **Some people believe that all you have to do is say no to temptation. But your willpower is no match for sin. The reality is, the more you try to say no by your own efforts, the worse it becomes. How does the apostle Paul describe his own experience with this in Romans 7:19?**

11. Paul's answer for victory over sin and the war within is found in saying yes to a *person*. He says in Romans 7:24–25: "O wretched man that I am! Who will deliver me from this body of death? I thank God—through Jesus Christ our Lord!" What does it mean to say YES to Jesus?

Holiness is all about becoming more and more like Jesus and it comes about when the veil of the law is removed (see 2 Cor. 3:14, 18). When the veil is removed, we see our beautiful Savior face-to-face and His glorious grace transforms us from glory to glory. The gospel of glorious grace always produces glorious lives as we behold Jesus.

KEY 3

VALUE THE PERSON OF JESUS

CHAPTER 11

GROW IN GRACE BY HEARING HIM

The opening story of the loving father, the beloved son, and the young man who was saved through the sacrifice of the son's life is a beautiful picture of the glorious gospel. Like the father in the story, God is looking for people who value and appreciate His Son. Whoever receives the Son receives all of God's blessings. To the one who values His Son, He gives every good thing He has. And how do we value His Son? One of the primary ways is by taking time to hear Him. Hear His words of grace to us and hear what He has done for us through His sacrifice at the cross.

1. What does Psalm 85:8 (NASB) tell us about what God is speaking to us?

2. How can you experience an increase in these *shalom* blessings in your body, family, career, and ministry?

Most of the focus in this chapter is derived from the accounts of what happened on the Mount of Transfiguration found in the Gospels of Matthew and Luke. We see how our Lord Jesus brought His disciples, Peter, James, and John, up a high mountain to pray. Scripture tells us that "as he was praying, the appearance of his face was transformed, and his clothes became dazzling white" (Luke 9:29 NLT). Then two of the most illustrious figures in the Jewish faith, Moses and Elijah, appeared and began talking with Jesus. Imagine the disciples' shock and awe when they saw these two great men—one representing the law and the other representing the prophets—appearing with Jesus in glory!

3. **What did Peter not realize when he blurted out, "Master, it is good for us to be here; and let us make three tabernacles: one for You, one for Moses, and one for Elijah" (Luke 9:33)?**

While Peter was still speaking, the bright cloud of the *shekinah* glory of God overshadowed them, and the Father's voice came out of the cloud, saying, "This is My beloved Son. Hear Him!" (Luke 9:35). When the disciples heard this, they hit the ground facedown, greatly afraid, and understandably so.

4. **To His absolutely terrified disciples, Jesus first words were, "Arise, and do not be afraid." What is so beautiful about these words and how do they reflect the nature of our Lord?**

5. **The Father said: "Hear *Him*," not "Hear *them*," referring to Moses, the lawgiver, and Elijah, who was not just an Old Testament prophet, but also the law-restorer (in the Old Testament, when Israel went after other gods, Elijah came to the people as the restorer of the law). As believers, what message should we take away from that?**

Never put Jesus—grace—on the same level as the law of Moses. The apostle Paul said, "But now the righteousness of God apart from the law is revealed, being witnessed by the Law and the Prophets, even the righteousness of God, through faith in Jesus Christ, to all and on all who believe" (Rom. 3:21–22). The revelation of the righteousness of God given to you as a gift apart from the law came through the Son. Therefore, "Hear HIM."

Today, no matter what you are facing in life, take time to hear Jesus.

6. **If you are concerned about symptoms in your body, what do you need to keep hearing?**

7. **If you are anxious about the needs and demands of tomorrow, what do you need to keep hearing?**

8. **If you've experienced the sting of betrayal, if you've been hurt by the words of people close to you, or if you are just feeling plain discouraged, what do you need to keep hearing?**

To really grow in grace and see its fruit manifest in our lives, we need to keep hearing the Son and His words of grace, because it is so easy to slide back into being law- or demand-conscious, as opposed to being grace- or supply-conscious. Hear Him today. Hear His words of grace!

9. When the collectors of the temple tax came to Peter and asked if Jesus paid the temple tax, he immediately responded, "Yes, He does" (Matt. 17:24–27). Rather than listen to Jesus, who was Peter listening to?

10. When James and John, who were also present at the transfiguration, saw how the Samaritans rejected Jesus, they said, "Lord, do You want us to command fire to come down from heaven and consume them, just as Elijah did?" (Luke 9:54). Who were they listening to, and what was Jesus' response?

There are many today still fighting for the voices of Moses and Elijah—the law and the prophets—not fully understanding that in the new covenant, it is all about hearing the voice of the resurrected Son of God. At the cross, He met all the righteous requirements of the law on our behalf and took upon Himself all the fiery judgment of God for our sins. His perfect sacrifice has fully satisfied God and silenced the law and the prophets. Today, we hear *Him!*

11. Why does the Father want us to hear only the Lord Jesus? Why are we to focus on Jesus and grow in the knowledge of His grace?

If you look at Scripture, you will see that while Moses and Elijah did mighty exploits, both great men of God still failed in the end. Toward the end of his life, Moses hit the rock twice in disobedience, yelled at the people, spoke unadvisedly out of anger and impatience, and wound up not being allowed to enter the promised land. And Elijah's ministry ended in depression and discouragement (see 1 Kings 19).

12. **In comparison, where the law and the prophets failed, what does the beautiful prophecy of the Messiah in Isaiah 42:1, 3–4 tell us?**

13. **The Father has spoken, "This is My beloved Son. Hear Him." Are you hearing Him today? What do you feel Jesus is saying to you as you study this chapter?**

Let His words of grace go deep into your heart and you can't help but be transformed from the inside out to walk in lasting breakthroughs and liberty.

CHAPTER 12

A REVOLUTION OF RELATIONSHIP

The grace revolution is all about Jesus. It is a revolution of God's amazing love, favor, restoration, and of people's lives transformed by a powerful encounter with our Lord Jesus. What our beloved Lord Jesus accomplished at Calvary has made all the difference. The cross put an end to the old covenant and kick-started the new covenant of grace.

The old covenant of law was about rules, religion, and regulations. The new covenant of grace is all about relationship. The old covenant of law created separation between God and His people; the new covenant of grace brings intimacy between God and His children. To understand the difference, take a look at what really happened when the law was given at Mount Sinai.

1. Before God's people had even heard the Ten Commandments, they proclaimed, "All that the LORD has spoken we will do" (Exod. 19:8). What does their statement reflect?

2. What warning did God give to the people at the foot of Mount Sinai?

3. The setting and scene where the Ten Commandments were given was terrifying and frightening to be at. How did God's people react to it?

The old covenant of the law was devoid of relationship. It was a covenant of distance and separation from God. The people were seized by fear and didn't want God to speak to them. That was and still is the effect of the law.

If we cling to the belief that we can be made righteous by our keeping of the Ten Commandments, we put ourselves at the foot of Mount Sinai. We will end up fearing God, conscious of His wrath, and unable to have an intimate relationship with Him. It also negates and shows we do not value, or have no understanding of, what our Lord Jesus' sacrifice at Calvary has accomplished to reconcile us to God and make us right before Him.

4. **What danger does the apostle Paul warn us about in Galatians 5:4 (NLT)?**

5. **God has moved mountains. He is no more on Mount Sinai, but has moved to Mount Zion. What is the difference between the two mountains?**

6. **Psalm 132:13–16 tells us that God has chosen Zion as His desired dwelling place, where He abundantly blesses with provisions, clothes with salvation, and saints shout aloud for joy. What does Psalm 125:1 promise? What does that mean for you?**

7. Hebrews 12:18, 22–23 tells us that we "have come to Mount Zion . . . to God the Judge of all, to the spirits of just men made perfect." Why can God judge us righteous and perfect on Mount Zion?

It was also on Mount Zion in Jerusalem that the Spirit of God came like a rushing mighty wind, filled the 120 disciples in the Upper Room, and the church was born (see Acts 2:2–4). The Spirit of God could not wait to inhabit the believers who had been justified by the blood of Jesus. Can you imagine, God living inside you? You are so near, you are of one spirit with God (see 1 Cor. 6:17) because our Lord Jesus first came near and gave His life for you.

8. The grace revolution is a revolution of relationship. What are you discovering about the relationship God wants to have with you that you may not have realized before?

The world we live in today is fraught with famine, economic uncertainty, corruption, and all kinds of evil and tragedies. Many people are living stressed, anxious lives just due to the chaos they see all around them. As Scripture says, the world will get darker, and it is (see Isa. 60:2).

But in the midst of all this darkness and uncertainty, Scripture speaks of a place of nearness to God where you and your family can take refuge in. "You shall dwell in the land of Goshen, and you shall be near to me, you and your children, your children's children, your flocks and your herds, and all that you have. There I will provide for you" (Gen. 45:10–11).

9. **What does the word *Goshen* mean? How does this comfort you as you see darkness and uncertainty in the world around you?**

10. **To be brought to this place of nearness to God and to be established on Mount Zion is to have an intimacy with God you never dreamed possible. What happens in this place of intimacy?**

11. **Adeline's testimony on pages 205–207 bears out how the grace revolution is a revolution of relationship and intimacy with God. What message from her story do you feel God is speaking to your heart?**

You can stay planted on Zion and in the place of nearness and intimacy with the Lord by being established in your righteous standing in Christ Jesus. Our Lord Jesus died on the cross and rose again on the third day to give us an everlasting righteousness that is anchored by faith in Him (see Rom. 4:5). And because you have His righteousness as a gift apart from your works, you can come boldly to the Father as His beloved son or daughter. You can enjoy fruitfulness instead of dead works when you live in the realm of His love for you, and not out of a sense of religious obligation.

12. **If you've been beaten down by negative circumstances, a long-term condition, or an addiction you can't seem to break, what hope does this give you?**

When Christ in His glorious grace is of full effect in your life, that breakthrough you have been believing for shall come to pass swiftly in the name of Jesus. That destructive addiction you have been battling for years will come crumbling down and no longer have a grip on your life. That health condition you have been trying to beat shall be no more. Amen!

CHAPTER 13

HAVING A HEART FOR JESUS

Six days before our Lord Jesus gave Himself up to be crucified, He gathered His friends together in Bethany, which was His home away from home. There, His closest friends, Martha, Mary, and Lazarus, loved Him, honored Him, and truly valued His presence. On His part, He cherished their company dearly, and always felt comfortable and relaxed with them. Though they had prepared a feast in His honor, it was overshadowed by the looming Passover. His friends understood to some degree what He intended to do, and their hearts were heavy because they cared deeply for Him.

As our Lord Jesus was eating, Mary brought out a jar of spikenard, a fragrant oil so costly that it was worth a whole year's wages. Not sparing a drop of her exquisite tribute, she anointed the Lord's feet and wiped them with her hair, filling the entire house with the opulent fragrance.

1. **What was it that Mary understood about Jesus that elicited such worship and a heart of a love for the Lord that could not be expressed in words?**

2. **In contrast to Mary, what was Judas Iscariot's reaction to what Mary did for Jesus? What does it tell you about his valuing of the Lord?**

3. Have you ever been told that reading the Bible or serving and being engaged in your local church is a waste of time? What oftentimes is the reason people make these accusations?

4. How do you test teachings and/or scriptural interpretations you hear to ensure that they reflect the estimation of our Lord Jesus that is due Him?

Ensuring we hear teachings that glorify the Lord Jesus above man's performance does not mean that we're saying performance in a believer's life is not important. The key to performance comes by the power of God's love, grace, and unmerited favor in your life! You will be able to perform when you know what the Lord has done for you and how you are perfectly loved.

5. How is this principle demonstrated in children who are bold, confident, and secure? What is their family life like?

6. At the same time, in an environment of love, grace, and affirmation, how are the child's parents also able to discipline, correct, and guide the child?

Some people have the erroneous idea that because we are under grace and highly favored children of God, there is no need for Him to correct and to discipline us. Yet Proverbs 3:12 (NLT) says, "For the LORD corrects those he loves, just as a father corrects a child in whom he delights."

7. No matter how we perform, what makes us highly favored by God?

8. As we grow in the grace and knowledge of our Lord Jesus Christ, our heavenly Father will correct, discipline, and guide us. But as we saw in chapter 10, He corrects us lovingly with His Word (see 2 Tim. 3:16), not by inflicting pain and suffering. Why is it so vital to experience the grace revolution and know that the heavenly Father only corrects us in love?

Judas Iscariot betrayed Jesus for thirty pieces of silver because he did not understand the value of Jesus. After the deed, he cried out in despair, "I have betrayed innocent blood" (Matt. 27:4 NIV). Then he went out and committed suicide. He rejected the Lord and his guilt drove him to hang himself.

9. Why do so many people today try to punish themselves for their own sins?

10. To anesthetize the voices of accusation in their own consciences, what do many people do? Has this also been your experience?

11. How can a person stop punishing himself and receive the abundant life that Jesus came to give?

12. **In Garrett's testimony on page 219, he told how his life went into a downward spiral of years of depression, drug and alcohol addiction, and despair, of losing his job, wife, and son, and growing to hate himself to the point where he attempted suicide. What completely turned his life around?**

If you've been bogged down in the mire of loneliness, discouragement, and self-destruction, don't waste another day in this dark place. Instead worship the One—our Lord and Savior, Jesus Christ—Who gave up everything and allowed Himself to be spat at, brutally beaten, and pierced with heavy nails at the cross for your redemption. Allow the fragrance of His love and His grace to flood every area of your life. Allow the perfume of His sacrifice to permeate and heal every hurt, every disappointment, and every insecurity.

13. **Write a prayer to the Lord, telling Him how you feel as you reflect on Who He is and what He has done because He loves you so. Thank Him for His grace that heals and overcomes everything destructive in your life.**

Our Lord Jesus has already paid the price for you to be whole and restored. He has already paid the price for you to come boldly and freely before His throne of grace. Oh, how He loves you! He loves you! He loves you!

We saw Mary's heart of worship for and Judas's heart of rejection toward Jesus unveiled in Bethany. In John 11:53, we see another response toward Jesus when He performed the astounding miracle of raising Lazarus from the dead. From that day on, it says the chief priests and the Pharisees plotted to kill Jesus—the One Who opened blind eyes, unstopped deaf ears, cleansed those with leprosy, and raised the dead!

14. What is so ironic about the chief priests and Pharisees wanting to destroy Jesus? What knowledge did they have, and yet also *not* have?

15. What warning can we take away from this regarding our own study and interpretation of the Scriptures?

16. What does true scriptural knowledge about Jesus lead you to?

Don't miss the Author when you are reading His Word.

17. In John 6:35, Jesus said, "I am the bread of life. He who comes to Me shall never hunger, and he who believes in Me shall never thirst." When you study the Bible, what does it mean "to feed on Christ" and what happens when you do?

Real holiness comes from beholding Jesus. As you behold our Lord, you are transformed from the inside out from glory to glory. When you value Jesus, your heart's desire is just to glorify Him in everything that you think, say, and do. When you have a heart for Jesus, everything in your life—whether it is your marriage, your parenting, or your career—will fall into place as you receive His finished work!

18. In the account in John 12, we saw Mary's beautiful heart of love and worship for the Lord. She poured out and gave her very best to the Lord, and the fragrance filled the house. What does that tell us about whatever we do for Jesus out of love for Him?

19. Jesus defended Mary against Judas's accusation that she wasted the costly oil of spikenard (see John 12:7). How does that reflect how Jesus values our worship?

In the Old Testament, the burnt offering came in three sizes—literally big, medium, and small (see Lev. 1:1–17). The rich would bring an expensive bullock; the middle-income, a lamb; and the poor, a pair of easy-to-obtain pigeons or turtledoves.

20. While the offerings differed in size, did God value them differently? Why?

21. How are these three animal sacrifices actually typologies of believers' appreciation of Jesus and His finished work today?

22. In the same way that all the three sacrifices were acceptable to the Lord, we as believers are all accepted in His sight. But God wants you to grow from having a pigeon-size revelation of His Son to having a bullock-size appreciation of Him. Why is this so important?

When you esteem Jesus, when you worship Him and give unto Him, it not only brings lasting transformation in your life, it also has a lasting effect for generations and generations to come. You will experience a quality of life beyond your wildest imagination when the Lord Jesus is at the center of it all. And that is why the grace revolution is all about having a heart for Jesus!

CHAPTER 14

FULLY POSSESS
THE FINISHED WORK

When you value the person of Jesus, you value what He values. Hebrews 10:24–25 tells us that our Lord greatly values and finds it very important that you be a part of a local church. While it is fantastic that you are receiving the gospel of grace through television, teaching resources, online materials, or even from this book, you need to be engaged in a church in your community. The grace revolution is not an isolated experience. It is best experienced in the context of a local church where there is fellowship, accountability, and wise counsel. The local church is not man's idea, it is God's idea, and indeed, there is something powerful about gathering together in an assembly of believers as part of the body of Christ where there is fellowship with *true possessors* of our Lord Jesus Christ.

The New Testament also contains warnings concerning people who verbally profess to be or call themselves Christians, but in actuality have never invited Jesus to be their personal Lord and Savior.

1. Second Peter 2:22 says, " 'A dog returns to his own vomit,' and, 'a sow, having washed, to her wallowing in the mire.' " This verse is often misquoted when a "Christian" is seen to have backslidden, turned away from the Lord, and is in danger of "losing his salvation." Does this verse refer to believers at all?

2. When a person is made a new creation in Christ Jesus, what changes?

If you have received the Lord Jesus into your life, I want you to know this beyond the shadow of any doubt: you are born again, you have received the gift of *eternal* life, your salvation is as secure as the promises in God's Word, you shall not come into judgment, and you have passed from death into life!

3. In Matthew 7:21–23, when Jesus said, "Not everyone who says to Me, 'Lord, Lord,' shall enter the kingdom of heaven, but he who does the will of My Father in heaven," was He referring to born-again believers?

4. Why is it so important to remove all confusion regarding the security of our salvation in Christ?

5. Jesus said in John 10:27–28, "My sheep hear My voice, and I know them, and they follow Me. And I give them eternal life, and they shall *never* perish; neither shall anyone snatch them out of My hand" (emphasis mine). What is so significant about the word translated "never"? What assurance does this give you?

The Bible tells us in no uncertain terms that "if you confess with your mouth the Lord Jesus and believe in your heart that God has raised Him from the dead, *you will be saved*" (Rom. 10:9, emphasis mine). It tells us that "*no one is able to snatch them out of My Father's hand*" (John 10:29, emphasis mine). The Bible tells us, "For God so loved the world that He gave His only begotten Son, that *whoever believes in Him should not perish but have everlasting life*" (John 3:16, emphasis mine). That's what the Bible says!

When the Golden Gate Bridge in San Francisco was being built in the 1930s, the enormous safety net that was installed below the bridge gave the workers the confidence to work more efficiently. Similarly, when we have the assurance of salvation and know that nothing can pluck us out of our Father's hand, it gives us confidence and strength to look to the Lord, to run the race better, and go from glory to glory. Christians who are secure in the Father's love will be transformed by the renewing of their minds with the power of God's amazing grace.

6. **Why is it that born-again believers established in God's grace want to live lives that glorify His holy name in every area of their lives?**

7. **Take some time and meditate on Titus 2:11–14: "For the grace of God that brings salvation has appeared to all men, teaching us that, denying ungodliness and worldly lusts, we should live soberly, righteously, and godly in the present age, looking for the blessed hope and glorious appearing of our great God and Savior Jesus Christ, who gave Himself for us, that He might redeem us from every lawless deed and purify for Himself His own special people, zealous for good works." What does this Scripture say is the result of being under grace and beholding the person of Jesus?**

Ephesians 1:6 tells us that by God's unearned, undeserved, and unmerited favor we have been made accepted in the Beloved—Jesus. This is true for every believer—by God's grace, you are accepted in the Beloved. The Greek word for "accepted" here is *charitoo,* which means "highly favored." Our Father in heaven wants you to know that you are *charitoo,* that is, highly favored in the Beloved. *Charitoo* also means "to compass with favor." In other words, we are *surrounded* with favor. This is our position in Christ: highly favored and surrounded by favor by the glory of His grace!

8. **By God's grace, we are accepted in the Beloved without labor. So what does 2 Corinthians 5:9 (KJV) mean when it says, "Wherefore we labor, that . . . we may be accepted of him"?**

9. **What is helpful for us to know about the Greek word *euarestos* or "well pleasing" in 2 Corinthians 5:9?**

10. **Illustrate how being "highly favored" and "well pleasing" are seen in the relationship between parents and children.**

It is the same in our relationship with our heavenly Father. When we know how much we are loved and are established in His grace, we want to do good works to bring delight to Him.

Everything we do today must flow from the lavish supply of God's grace. Our giving has to be out of His grace. Our serving has to be out of His grace. When His grace is our delight, we can't help but labor more abundantly and bring delight to our Father's heart!

11. According to 1 Corinthians 15:10, what motivated the apostle Paul to work harder than all the other apostles for the gospel's sake?

12. In Jayden's testimony on page 243, how did the discovery that he was God's beloved change how he desired to please God in practical living?

13. Take a moment to think about the story of the father of the prodigal son (see Luke 15:11–32). How does it make you feel like responding when you consider that our loving, caring, smiling Father runs to us when we've failed?

The grace revolution begins from the inside and flows to the outside, and is about always being loved and highly favored by the Father.

KEY 4

SPEAK THE LANGUAGE OF FAITH

CHAPTER 15

LOVE LIFE AND SEE GOOD DAYS

Your words are powerful. What you speak over yourself can change your life. God's Word is so beautifully clear: "For 'He who would love life and see good days, let him refrain his tongue from evil, and his lips from speaking deceit'" (1 Pet. 3:10). If you desire to love life and see good days, all you need to do is to refrain your tongue from speaking evil. It sounds simple. In fact, you may even contend that it is *too* simple.

But the Bible reminds us not to despise the tongue simply because it is small: "Look also at ships: although they are so large and are driven by fierce winds, they are turned by a very small rudder wherever the pilot desires. Even so the tongue is a little member and boasts great things" (James 3:4–5). In the book of Proverbs, Solomon also declares, "Death and life are in the power of the tongue, and those who love it will eat its fruit" (Prov. 18:21). It is evident that God does not want you to underestimate the power of your words!

1. **Do you truly believe that your words wield so much influence and power over all your life? Reflect on the words you habitually speak. Are they words that bring life and blessing to your own situations and to other people? What would you like to change about what you say?**

Read 1 Peter 3:8–10. The apostle Peter's quote was made in the context of our relationships with people. As we have been transformed by the gospel of grace from the inside out in our relationship with God, that grace that we have experienced is meant to overflow into all our earthly relationships like a mighty tidal wave.

2. **What type of people does Peter say we should be in our relationships?**

3. **In 1 Peter 3:9, the original Greek word for "blessing" is *eulogeo*, which means "to speak well of" and is where we get the English word "eulogy." What simple but amazingly powerful principle is stated here?**

4. **Take some time and meditate on how you have the power to bless and to be a blessing everywhere you go. Do not underestimate the difference this will make in your life and in the lives of others. What are some of the ways you can practice speaking well of something or of the people in your life?**

Every time you speak His blessings over your life, you are taking possession of your blessed place in Christ.

The scriptural opposite of speaking well is to curse. When our Lord cursed the fig tree, did He say, "I curse you, fig tree"? No, He simply said, "Let no one eat fruit from you ever again" (Mark 11:14). And the next day, when the disciples passed by the fig tree again, Peter said, "Rabbi, look! The fig tree which You *cursed* has withered away" (Mark 11:21, emphasis mine). Although Jesus didn't use the word *curse*, He also did not correct Peter because he was right—*the negative words spoken were tantamount to a curse.*

5. **What incredibly important principle does this illustrate about our words?**

Don't miss this! Change your words, and change your life. Flush out the negative words in your life with the words of God's grace, love, and power!

6. **Now that you know words of defeat, bitterness, anger, and complaint are toxic and tantamount to a curse, how will this affect what you choose to say, for example about your presently negative situation, or your future?**

7. **Note that when Jesus first spoke to the fig tree, it did not wither away instantly. What encouragement does this give us when we speak to our challenge and nothing seems to happen?**

8. **Lorraine's wonderful testimony (page 255) shows you the power of praying or speaking, and how change begins from the first day you speak. Why did she plead the blood of the Lamb of God over this situation?**

Today, we can declare that no plague, no death, no punishment, no harm, no danger, no evil can come near our dwelling because the full payment for our sins has already been made by our Lord Jesus.

Now take a moment and read what the apostle Paul says in Romans 10:4–6, 8–10 about the power of speaking in the new covenant of grace as he contrasts it to the old covenant. Please note that Christ marks the end of the law and the beginning of the new covenant, and there is no mixing of the two. Today, God only deals with us according to the new covenant.

9. **What are the vital differences Paul notes between the two covenants, and what difference does the power of right believing make?**

A person transformed by grace not only keeps the law of God outwardly, but His heart is full of Jesus. He overflows with generosity, he is passionate for his spouse, and he is zealous for good works and the glory of His Savior, Jesus Christ. See the difference? It's like night and day.

10. Your words are powerful. In Romans 10:8, the apostle Paul added that the word of faith is near you, "in your mouth and in your heart." What does that tell you about the progression of words of faith?

11. It is so important that under the new covenant you are not working for your own righteousness in order to be healed and blessed. Compare Romans 10:5 and 10:6. What is the focus of the law versus the righteousness of faith?

The righteousness of the law doeth, but the righteousness of faith speaketh (see Rom. 10:5–6 KJV). Therefore, speak! Open your mouth and speak! Faith (believing) is released by speaking.

You and I are made in the image of God, Who, when things were very dark at the beginning of creation, didn't speak about the darkness He saw. No, God spoke forth what He wanted to see. He said, "Let there be light," and there was light (see Gen. 1:3–4). God saw light *after* He spoke it.

12. We serve a God "who gives life to the dead and calls those things which do not exist as though they did" (Rom. 4:17). How is that seen in the changing of Abraham's name (see Gen. 17:5), the healing of the man with the withered hand (see Matt. 12:10–13), and the healing of the man who had an infirmity for thirty-eight years (see John 5:5–9)?

You are made in God's image. The same can and will happen for you when you see and speak what you believe and want to see! Do you want to love life and see good days? Then start speaking it before you even see it.

In the new covenant, God wants us to focus on believing and speaking. You may be faced with darkness, barrenness, sickness, or infirmity, but speak by faith what you want to see. God saw the darkness, but spoke what He wanted to see. So what do you want to see in your life—in your body, your marriage, your children, your family, your household, and your place of employment? Remember it's not about what you *currently see*, but what you *want to see.*

13. **It is unfortunate that the enemy has been successful in deceiving many people into speaking negatively, often with bitterness and unforgiveness, over their own lives and the lives of those around them. Read Proverbs 14:30 (AMP). What does that warn us about holding on to negative emotions?**

14. **As difficult as it often is to forgive someone who has committed an injustice against us and does not deserve it, why should we still choose to bless them (see 1 Pet. 3:9)?**

15. **The Jewish people have a salutation when they propose a toast. They say, "*L'chaim,*" which means, "To life!" How will you start to use your words to celebrate and step into the abundant life that our Lord came to bring us?**

When you change your words, you will change your life. *L'chaim!*

CHAPTER 16

THE POWER OF IDENTITY

Read the story of the businessman and the beggar. This story highlights the power of identity. The businessman gave this beggar a renewed sense of meaning and identity by simply speaking over him and calling forth a latent potential that was in him. By calling this beggar a businessman, he awakened in him a renewed sense of worth, value, and importance. The words gave the beggar a new perspective—a new belief and vision—that propelled him to walk away from the lie that a beggar was all he could be. This story has parallels for believers today.

1. Why do so many believers struggle with sin, addictions, and destructive bondages?

2. When the Corinthian church had fallen into sin, Paul didn't point these believers back to the law of Moses. What did he remind them of in 1 Corinthians 6:15, 19–20 (KJV)?

3. What is the best way to encourage and lift up believers whom you know are struggling with sin? How can you practice this principle in your own life?

The moving praise report from Melissa on pages 265–268 describes the journey that she took to discover her true identity in Christ. Melissa grew up being told and feeling that she was a worthless nobody. Without having the love of her father, she desperately sought love in many relationships and partners, which led to a destructive lifestyle of sin, and feelings of deep unhappiness, confusion, and constant emptiness. A person who believes they are truly a worthless nobody will start behaving as if they are a valueless and worthless nobody. That is the negative power of wrong believing.

4. **What did Melissa believe about God as a result of what she'd been told about Him?**

5. **What did she discover about God that totally transformed her from the inside out?**

6. **What have Melissa's repeated confessions of her righteousness in Christ done for her?**

Hollywood and the secular media have deified and glamorized the party lifestyle—drinking, getting high, and sleeping around—as cool and carefree. Melissa's story peels back the curtains on the lie that the YOLO life—the you-only-live-once, consequence-free existence—is awesome. You see how deeply unhappy and depressed these people entangled in a sinful lifestyle are. Yet our teenagers and youths are being bombarded with these images on their social media channels, in movies, and on television shows, where sinful lifestyles are not only tolerated but also celebrated.

7. **Many churches have responded to this by preaching more on the law, repentance, and character. What do young people hear in those messages?**

8. **When the church proclaims, "We love the sinner but hate the sin," what message do those who are struggling with sinful lifestyles actually hear?**

9. **In chapter 9, and here again, we see Jesus, "the friend of sinners" (see Matt. 11:19), reaching out to and rescuing sinners, and how just one encounter with His love and grace caused them to be transformed forever from the inside out. What was His attitude toward their sin, and what does real grace do for sinners?**

God's glorious grace opens the prison doors for those trapped in sin and bondage. He has given you the power to walk out freely today. Welcome His deep love for you and you will be set free!

The grace revolution begins with a person and His name is Jesus. Romans 8:3 says, "For what the law could not do in that it was weak through the flesh, God did by sending His own Son" (Rom. 8:3). The answer is not found in the law, but in the Son. When you have Jesus as your Lord and Savior, you have everything. You have, most importantly, a new and righteous identity in Christ.

10. **Quite often, a person can experience a breakthrough but not experience lasting change in that area of struggle. Why? What are they forgetting?**

11. **Why is it so essential for you to be part of a local church?**

I have a word in season for you, and I want to challenge you to cultivate a robust revelation of your righteous identity in Christ by repeatedly confessing your righteousness in Christ. Throughout the day, whether you are driving to work, shopping for groceries, or preparing a meal for your family, just say quietly under your breath, "I am the righteousness of God in Christ. All the promises, blessings, and protection that belong to the righteous are mine" (see Prov. 10:6). This is the key for you to experience lasting breakthroughs in your life!

12. **If you truly desire to see more breakthroughs in your life and experience the power to live above defeat, how can you speak faith regarding who you truly are in Christ?**

CHAPTER 17

RELEASE THE POWER TO REIGN

The story of the Shunammite woman (see 2 Kings 4:8–37) is a powerful account that we can all learn something from. Confronting the toughest challenge of her life, she held back the turmoil in her heart over the death of her child and spoke contrary to her natural circumstances. Outwardly everything was not well. Yet she kept saying to herself and the people around her, "It is well. It is well." She didn't speak what she saw; she spoke what she wanted to see. She kept her eyes and her faith on God, and believed with all her heart that in God, all things were well and would work out for her good.

1. You may be going through some adversity in your life right now. Perhaps you have suffered a loss, or are going through a very challenging season. Be encouraged by this story. What can you start to believe to strengthen yourself in the Lord?

Know that because you are the Lord's, you can stand firm and strong upon His faithfulness to bring healing and restoration in your life.

2. Why can we stand firm, stand strong, and stand proud upon the promises of God, and speak, "It is well" over every area of our lives?

3. We can all learn to stand firm upon God's promises. For instance, Proverbs 11:21 (KJV) says, "The seed of the righteous shall be delivered." This means that your sons and daughters shall be kept safe and protected in Jesus' name. How can you stand firm upon this promise for your children, especially when you are worried for their safety?

Romans 5:17 says, "Much more those who receive abundance of grace and of the gift of righteousness will reign in life through the One, Jesus Christ." Unfortunately, some people believe that receiving is too simplistic and insubstantial. Their focus is on doing, on duty, on what is man's responsibility. Don't ever underestimate the power of receiving. Man's greatest doing—his greatest duty and greatest responsibility—is to humble himself to receive from the Lord Jesus!

4. Martha and Mary are classic examples of this truth (see Luke 10:38–42). Contrast these two types of believers.

Who would you say you are more like? In what ways?

5. What was Martha missing, and what was Jesus' gracious response?

6. Because Mary did the one thing needful—sitting at the Lord's feet and just receiving from her Savior—she ended up performing the right service for Him. We read in John 12:1–8 that she anointed the Lord with costly fragrant oil for His burial. All the other women who wanted to anoint Him for His burial were too late on resurrection morning (see Luke 24:1–3). Mary was able to do the right thing at the right time because she kept her heart centered on receiving from the Lord. How can we do the same?

In chapter 5, we saw that if you believe you must confess every sin you commit in order to be forgiven, it will put you under an impossible standard to live by and on a never-ending treadmill that leads to perpetual sin-consciousness. It will also make you more susceptible to temptations because you are constantly feeling like a dirty sinner. Conversely, when you know that you have the forgiveness of sins and that the payment of our Lord Jesus' blood has perfectly washed you clean, you can openly talk to your Father about your failings and mistakes with no sin debt on your conscience and receive His grace and help to break free from the cycle of sin.

7. There is a teaching that attempts to segment God's forgiveness, arguing that there is a difference between "judicial forgiveness" and "parental forgiveness." Read pages 285–286 closely. How does this teaching lead to the same bondage as what we studied in chapter 5?

8. Acts 13:38–39 declares, "Through this Man is preached to you the forgiveness of sins; and by Him everyone who believes is justified from *all* things from which you could not be justified by the law of Moses" (emphasis mine). Did the apostle Paul make distinctions in forgiveness? What did he preach?

The Word of God states you have been and you continue to be forgiven. Amen! In your darkest moments, and even when you have failed, you can say with boldness, "I *am* the righteousness of God in Christ. I *have* forgiveness of sins, and God loves me and is for me. It is well with my soul!"

Remember, the righteousness of faith speaks! The Bible exhorts us by saying, "Let the weak say, 'I am strong' " (Joel 3:10). Faith always speaks what it wants to see, not what it currently sees. Faith is "the substance of things hoped for, the evidence of things not seen" (Heb. 11:1).

9. **When you are weak, what promise from God can you speak?**

10. **When there is sickness in your body, what promise from God can you speak?**

11. **When there is lack in your life, what promise from God can you speak?**

12. **In the midst of a struggle with a bad habit or addiction, what promise from God can you speak?**

13. **In Jimmy's testimony on page 291, what happened when he began to actively confess by faith his righteousness in Christ?**

Lay hold of this gift of righteousness that you have through Christ and speak it boldly. You'll start experiencing the power to live above defeat and begin to see any bondage—no matter how long you may have had it—lose its hold over your life. This is what the grace revolution is all about.

KEY 5

RECEIVE HIS ABUNDANT RESTORATION

CHAPTER 18

RECEIVE GOD'S MUCH-MORE RESTORATION

Jeremiah 23:4 tells us, " 'I will set up shepherds over them who will feed them; and they shall fear no more, nor be dismayed, nor shall they be lacking,' says the LORD." In the grace revolution, God Himself is setting up shepherds who will preach the gospel of grace with authority and impart to the hearers security, certainty, assurance, and confidence so they will no longer be oppressed by fear or discouragement! If you have lost many years living in doubt, fear, and depression, God is restoring those lost years to you in the grace revolution.

1. **When the Lord restores to you whatever the enemy has stolen from you, it is always greater in quantity or quality. Based upon the principle of restitution in the trespass offering found in Leviticus 5 and 6, how much restoration can we look to the Lord for?**

2. **Notice that the person brings his restitution on the day of his trespass offering. What is the trespass offering a picture of?**

3. Because you have accepted Christ as your trespass offering, what beautiful promise of God's much-more restoration is coming your way (see Joel 2:25–26)?

Because of what our Lord Jesus has done for us on the cross, you can believe for total and complete restoration—for God to redeem ALL the time that has been lost and wasted!

4. On pages 298–299, Clarence's phenomenal testimony illustrates how God restores all that the locust has eaten. What was restored to Clarence when he embraced the grace of our Lord and God as his Dad?

5. God restored to Clarence what all the years of drug addiction took from him. For others it is a restoration from years of being bound by shackles of legalism. What are you believing for God to restore in your life today?

6. Our Lord Jesus said: "If you abide in My word, you are My disciples indeed. And you shall know the truth, and the truth shall make you free. . . . Therefore if the Son makes you free, you shall be free indeed" (John 8:31–32, 36). Is "the truth" that sets us free the old covenant of law? What did our Lord really mean?

The apostle Peter established what the truth that sets us free is in Acts 15, where you find the account of the Jerusalem Council convening to debate which of the old covenant laws should be imposed on Gentile believers. Note Acts 15:8–9, where Peter says that when the Gentiles simply put their faith in the Lord Jesus for the forgiveness of their sins (see Acts 10:43–44), they were filled with the Holy Spirit in the same way as the Jewish believers. Hence, this truth, that those who believe in Jesus will receive forgiveness of their sins, is what truly sets you free to receive God's abiding presence and His blessings. Peter explained that the Gentiles heard him preach the forgiveness of sins, *believed* the good news, and had their hearts purified by faith.

7. At the Jerusalem Council, what did Peter say about *how* the hearts of the Gentile believers were purified? What led to the purification of their hearts (which also leads to the purification of our hearts)?

8. If someone tells you that in order to have a pure heart you need to do this and that, according to God's Word, what unshakable confidence can you have concerning your salvation, your relationship with the Lord, and seeing restoration happen for you?

After the apostle Peter told the Jerusalem Council that God had purified the hearts of the Gentiles by faith, he added, "Now therefore, why do you test God by putting a yoke on the neck of the disciples which neither our fathers nor we were able to bear?" (Acts 15:10). That "yoke" that Peter described as unbearable and impossible to keep is the old covenant law.

9. **In Matthew 11:28–30, what did the Lord Jesus tell all the Jewish people who were under that heavy yoke of the law to do?**

10. **In the gospel of grace, what does Jesus promise He will give us? What does that have to do with our restoration?**

And here's more. When our Lord stood in the synagogue in Nazareth, He was handed the book of Isaiah and He found the place where it was written: "The Spirit of the Lord is upon Me, because He has anointed Me to preach the gospel to the poor; He has sent Me to heal the brokenhearted, to proclaim liberty to the captives and recovery of sight to the blind, to set at liberty those who are oppressed; to proclaim the acceptable year of the Lord" (Luke 4:18–19). Now pay close attention to what our Lord did next: "Then He closed the book. . . . And He began to say to them, 'Today this Scripture is fulfilled in your hearing'" (Luke 4:20–21).

11. **To understand why our Lord closed the book of Isaiah after He read the portion, what do we see when we look at the Scripture He was quoting from in fuller context?**

Our Lord's "acceptable year" speaks of the dispensation, time, and season that we are in. We are not in the age of "the day of vengeance." That day will come, and our Lord will return to deliver Israel from total destruction and judge the earth. But the age that we live in today is the age of grace. We are under the dispensation of grace.

12. **The Greek word for "acceptable" here is *dektos*. What does it mean that we are living in the *dektos* season?**

13. **How does knowing that you are in the *dektos* season bring rest to your heart right now?**

14. **How does knowing that you are in the *dektos* season affect what you can expect from Him in a specific area of need today?**

We just witnessed how precise our Lord is in rightly dividing God's Word. Once He proclaimed the *dektos* year, He shut the book. He declared that at that precise moment in Nazareth, Isaiah's prophecy was being fulfilled. The age of grace had come. He did not mix the old covenant of law with the new covenant of grace.

15. What happens when someone mixes the covenant of law with grace?

16. When you learn to rightly divide God's Word, as the apostle Paul said to his young apprentice, Timothy, in 2 Timothy 2:15, you will begin to see the Lord's grace, His love, and His security flood every area of your life. In Valerie's testimony on page 310, what amazing results happened when she began to learn how to rightly divide God's Word?

Remember, the grace revolution is a revolution of restoration. Jesus shut the book! This is the age of glorious grace! This is your time to walk in liberty, peace, restoration, and joy in the acceptable year of the Lord!

CHAPTER 19

LIVE WITH FULL ASSURANCE OF FAITH

The *now word* for the grace revolution is found in Jeremiah 23:4, where the Lord says, "I will set up shepherds over them who will feed them; and they shall fear no more, nor be dismayed, nor shall they be lacking." This is happening all over the world today. God is setting up shepherds who care for, nourish, and feed His sheep, not beat, threaten, and intimidate them.

As we've seen, the grace revolution is a revolution of restoration of everything the enemy has stolen—your health, your provision, your confidence, even your meaning and purpose in life. Our Father in heaven will restore to you and rebuild you from the inside out.

1. Does it make you excited to know we're living in the days Jeremiah 23 talks about? What areas do you want to see yourself *not fearing, not being dismayed,* and *not lacking* in?

2. Take a moment to read and be amazed and inspired by the testimony of restoration from Marcus (page 314). Prior to his encounter with our Lord Jesus through the gospel of grace, what had been his view of God and healing?

After Marcus discovered what our Lord Jesus had done for Him on the cross and especially His love for him even when he had messed up, he experienced the profusely abundant favor of God in every area of his life. He shared that there was "such a huge comfort and assurance," a very appropriate choice of words because *the grace revolution is a revolution of assurance and peace*. The gospel of peace imparts deep shalom-peace, comfort, and rest to the innermost recesses of our troubled hearts (see Rom. 10:15).

3. Take some time to meditate on this Scripture: "Let us draw near with a true heart in full assurance of faith, having our hearts sprinkled from an evil conscience and our bodies washed with pure water" (Heb. 10:22). What does our heavenly Father want us to have great assurance of?

So what is the foundation we can stand on to have the "full assurance of faith"? Hebrews 10 provides three *W*'s that work together to give us this full assurance of faith, which is given line-upon-line teaching starting on page 319. Please read it carefully as we cover the main points here.

Hebrews 10 makes it clear that the law and all its many different types of offerings were only shadows of the substance—our Lord Jesus Christ. His perfect offering on the cross is the only offering that could take away all our sins once and for all (see Heb. 10:4, 10). Always remember that under the first covenant, *the law always disqualifies you the moment you fail at any point*.

4. The first *W* is the *will of the Father*. What does Hebrews 10:9 tell us the will of the Father is?

Our Lord Jesus, the very personification of grace, came and qualified us by taking our sin upon Himself at the cross! He took away the first covenant (that disqualified God's people) so that He might establish the second—the new and better covenant of grace. Hallelujah!

Hebrews 10:11–12 goes on to say that "every priest" under the old covenant "stands ministering daily and offering repeatedly the same sacrifices, which can never take away sins. But this Man, after He had offered one sacrifice for sins forever, sat down at the right hand of God." Because the work of the Old Testament priests was never finished, they remained standing and ministering daily, offering sacrifice after sacrifice that could never take away sins. Our Lord's work, on the other hand, was so perfect in removing our sins once and for all that He could sit down at the Father's right hand. This is the second *W*—the *work of the Son*.

5. **By His one sacrifice at the cross, our Lord *completely finished* the job of removing *all* our sins, so that we can come freely to the Father to receive mercy and grace from Him, even when we have failed, to reign over our failures. How does this put strength and hope in your heart today?**

Today, find your security in the work of the Son. You are forgiven and made righteous in Christ *once and for all* by His blood.

Let's recap. The first *W* that provides a foundation we can stand on to have the "full assurance of faith" is the *will of the Father*. The second *W* is the *work of the Son*. Now, in Hebrews 10:15, 17, we come to the third *W*—the *witness of the Holy Spirit* to us that "their sins and their lawless deeds I will remember no more." All three persons of the Godhead—the Father, Son, and Holy Spirit—are involved in giving us assurance of faith regarding the forgiveness of our sins.

6. **The Holy Spirit, the third person of the Godhead, dwells in all believers today. What cornerstone truth has He, the Spirit of truth and the Comforter, been sent to *witness* to you?**

7. **We have the Holy Spirit to *witness* to us the *will of the Father* and the *work of the Son*. How does this give you assurance of faith?**

8. When we are led by the Holy Spirit, what does He constantly remind and assure us of?

9. Proverbs 24:16 says, even though "a righteous man may fall seven times," he will "rise again." Where does the power to rise come from?

Take a few moments to meditate on the roles of the Holy Spirit as stated in John 16:8–11: "And when He [the Holy Spirit] has come, He will convict the world of sin, and of righteousness, and of judgment: of sin, because they do not believe in Me; of righteousness, because I go to My Father and you see Me no more; of judgment, because the ruler of this world is judged."

10. When someone says, based upon these verses, that one of the Holy Spirit's roles is to convict believers of sin, how are they misquoting the Scriptures?

11. Before we became born-again believers, the Holy Spirit convicted us of the sin of unbelief in Christ. Once we become believers, what important thing does John 16:8–11 tell us that the Holy Spirit convicts us of?

12. When you are established in the *will* of the Father, the *work* of the Son, and the *witness* of the Holy Spirit, you will experience the full assurance of faith that Hebrews 10:22 talks about. The grace revolution is the end of being insecure, always fearful, and forever wondering if you have done enough for God. Based on what you have learned in this chapter, take a moment to reflect on how you can start living every day with full assurance of faith and boldness to draw near to God.

Beloved and righteous one, get ready to receive your breakthrough and restoration in Christ today!

CHAPTER 20

THE GRACE REVOLUTION IS HERE

In Jeremiah 23:4, we see the message to be preached in this day and hour of the grace revolution. Our Chief Shepherd showed me that when pastors and leaders preach the unadulterated gospel of grace, their flocks will "fear no more, nor be dismayed, nor shall they be lacking." If you are under God-appointed leadership, these are the blessings of God's grace you should be experiencing.

In speaking to me about what I should feed His people with in this hour, the Lord gave me Jeremiah 23:5–6: " 'Behold, the days are coming,' says the LORD, 'that I will raise to David a Branch of righteousness; a King shall reign and prosper, and execute judgment and righteousness in the earth. In His days Judah will be saved, and Israel will dwell safely; now this is His name by which He will be called: THE LORD OUR RIGHTEOUSNESS.' "

1. **The revelation of the grace revolution is "THE LORD OUR RIGHTEOUS-NESS"—highlighted in full capitalization! In Hebrew it is *Jehovah-Tsidkenu*. It is the Holy Spirit's way of saying, "Don't miss this. Seeing this will change your life!" Based on the above Scriptures, what three effects will you experience as you believe and grow in the revelation of THE LORD OUR RIGHTEOUSNESS?**

John 4 records our Lord's encounter with the Samaritan woman at the well, a broken woman who had had five divorces and was living with a man who wasn't her husband. To this woman who was entangled in a life of sin, the Lord used the language of everyday things and simple, practical illustrations to gently restore her dignity to her and rebuild her broken life. At the end of her encounter with Jesus, this Samaritan woman ended up completely changed and transformed by the Lord's love and grace. After encountering Jesus she became an evangelist in the city, going about saying, "Come, see a Man who told me all things that I ever did" (John 4:29), and "many of the Samaritans of that city believed in Him because of the word of the woman" (John 4:39).

2. **What about you? What will you do with the gospel of grace and person of Jesus Who has been introduced to you in this book?**

Today the grace revolution is led by precious people just like the woman at the well—imperfect people whose lives have been transformed and restored after an authentic encounter with our Lord Jesus Christ. Once they have tasted for themselves His abundant grace and gift of righteousness, their lives are never the same again, and they can't help but proclaim, "Come, see a Man!" and point people to the Savior!

3. Why should you not be intimidated by anyone using high-sounding theological words to try to dismiss the gospel of glorious grace?

4. Edwina's testimony on page 341 bears many similarities to the Samaritan woman's story. What struck Edwina the most when she first heard the gospel of grace and encountered Jesus that is exactly what the woman at the well experienced?

5. What amazing encouragement can we receive from our Lord's kindness to the Samaritan woman?

The truth is, you *are,* right now, the righteousness of God through Jesus' precious blood. You can have a true and intimate relationship with the Lord because when you confess your sins, it is not *in order to be forgiven*; you confess your sins, knowing that you have *already been forgiven*, and that you are having conversations with THE LORD YOUR RIGHTEOUSNESS. There is a huge difference!

6. **Some people say that grace is basic and good for new believers, but that one has to mature into more "advanced" things like holiness and repentance. According to Galatians 4:1–7 and Hebrews 5:13, what is the revelation that marks a mature son or daughter of God?**

Peter's relationship with the Lord Jesus over the years reveals the true maturity that God desires for us—a growing revelation of His grace and forgiveness. In chapter 2, we saw that in one of Peter's first encounters with the Lord (see Luke 5:8), Peter was most conscious of the Lord's holiness, not His love, in contrast with his own unworthy state of sinfulness. That was followed by Peter's discipleship and closeness to Jesus as well as his restoration and deep assurance of Jesus' love after his denial of the Lord (see Luke 22:34).

7. **Now, in John 21, we see the Lord restoring Peter, this time to *ministry*. What caused Peter to plunge into the water and swim toward Jesus? Was it the Lord's holiness or His grace?**

What Peter experienced is what so many people are experiencing around the world in the grace revolution. They are receiving a restoration of the assurance that they can come boldly before their Lord in the throne room of grace, even when they have failed!

8. **Meditate on how the Lord Himself is your righteousness, today and forevermore. Is it imparting peace, assurance, faith, and boldness to your heart? Why? How do you now see your life and your future knowing this?**

My friend, the grace revolution is not about a movement, teaching, or doctrine. It is all about our Lord Jesus. It is He Who brings about the inside-out transformation of countless lives to the glory of His name. It is He Who brings about God's much-more restoration, putting an end to wasted years, lost health, estranged relationships, and shattered dreams, and bringing in fresh, new beginnings.

In our systematic study of the truths established through the five keys in *Grace Revolution*, I pray that you have enjoyed growing in your revelation of our beautiful Lord Jesus and His glorious grace. I hope that your reflections throughout this book have opened your eyes to see His love and grace for you and given you the confidence to face life because of all He has done for you at the cross.

As you've made your way through and come to the end of this study guide, I pray that the powerful truths of God's forgiveness and gift of righteousness will go deep into your heart, establish you in the security of your eternal salvation, and liberate you from every kind of defeat. Above all, I hope this journey you've taken is releasing you to have the closest, most loving relationship you could ever ask for with your heavenly Father. That even now you are experiencing the sweetness of falling in love with our Lord Jesus as you lean in to His love for you and are already experiencing the grace revolution personally. Beloved, as you keep receiving His grace for you, expect your mind to be continually renewed, your body to be healed, and your life to be infused with His wonderful presence, peace, and victory!

ANSWERS

CHAPTER 1

2. Dean realized that grace is not about what he deserved, but all about the Lord's love and the unearned, unmerited favor that He gives freely without demanding anything.

3. Dean was full of guilt, believing that God wanted him to suffer for his mistakes and repeated failures, carry his own punishment, and that he would never have love, favor, and acceptance in this life because of those mistakes.

4. Dean stated: "... all I had to do was to focus on Jesus' finished work on the cross and keep my eyes and ears open to His gospel, the good news of grace ... this truth sets one free. I began to realize that grace is undeserved favor and there was nothing I could ever do to earn or re-earn this unmerited favor in my life, regardless of my sins or efforts to make things right. I began to realize that I am highly favored and accepted in the beloved family of my Lord."

UNDER LAW	UNDER GRACE
My focus is on what I need to accomplish for God	My focus is on what **Jesus** has accomplished for me
I am disqualified by my disobedience	I am qualified by **Jesus' obedience**
I am made righteous (or justified) only by my works/only when I do right	I am made righteous or justified by faith when I believe right
I am constantly demand-conscious, because the law demands righteousness from me	I can be supply-conscious, because **Jesus supplies** righteousness as a gift to me

8. God's Word is so clear: when you are under grace and not under the law, sin shall NOT have dominion over you. You cannot be under grace and not be holy any more than you can be underwater and not be wet! It is being under grace that gives you the power to live a victorious life.

CHAPTER 2

1. Peter was blown away by the unprecedented catch of fish the Lord gave him and his crew. He never imagined he would bring in such a great haul which was why he only let down one net. What Peter witnessed made him kneel before Jesus and proclaim, "Depart from me, for I am a sinful man, O Lord!" (Luke 5:8). His experiencing the undeserved goodness of God brought him to a place of repentance.

2. *God's blessing* in the form of a huge load of fish (when Peter had caught nothing the night before) came first. This tells us that under the new covenant of grace, God blesses us first, and His blessings, favor, and overflowing love lead us to repentance (see Rom. 2:4)!

3. No one tries to clean himself before he takes a bath. Jesus *is* the bath! He is the Savior. Come to Him with all your inadequacies, all your addictions, all your habits, and all your hang-ups, and let Him do what He does best. Let Him save you and restore you to wholeness!

4. *Teshuvah* means "Because of the cross of Jesus, return to grace." Repentance is all about returning to God's grace because of His goodness demonstrated at the cross of Jesus. It is not about returning to the law of Moses. It is about turning to the cross and returning to His grace. His grace is your source of power and strength over every sin.

5. Repent by turning to the cross—see that mistake punished in the body of Jesus—and return to God's grace by receiving His unmerited favor to overcome this area of weakness.

7. God's Word proclaims that "sin shall not have dominion over you, for you are not under law but under grace" (Rom. 6:14). True grace swallows up the destructive powers of sin. The scriptural way for a person to overcome the power of sin is through God's glorious grace. They only get liberated and transformed when they encounter the love of their Savior!

8. If someone's life has been impacted by Jesus' unconditional love and sacrifice, they will always be looking for a way out of sin and its painful, destructive consequences. They will not be trying to find ways or excuses to sin. Through the power of our Lord and Savior, Jesus Christ, sin no longer dominates people and true repentance occurs when people receive and believe the gospel of grace! *Grace* is the truth that sets people *free* (see John 8:32).

9. Robert said, "I heard Pastor Prince preach a sermon where he said that the solution was to quit trying to win on my own and to confess to the Lord, 'Lord, I cannot, but You can.' This became my motto and I quit trying to quit using tobacco. I no longer stayed buried under guilt and condemnation. I believed and confessed that even though I was struggling with this tobacco habit, God still loves me no less and that Jesus' finished work still avails for me."

10. At the point of writing his testimony, every time an urge popped up, Robert practiced turning to the cross and returning to grace. He said, "I say to the Lord that I know His grace and what He has for me are much better than tobacco, and the urge leaves."

12. If you've been trying to quit a habit, turn to the cross and return to the truths of God's grace—that what our Lord Jesus has done for you at the cross is so much greater than all your failings, and that because of His perfect, finished work, you are still deeply loved, highly favored, and greatly blessed. When you let such a revelation of God's grace wash over your heart again and again, you can't help but deeply appreciate what the Lord has done for you and how His grace has set you apart to shine for His glory. You won't want to continue in sin. Instead, you will find His power causing you to increasingly overcome any sin that has been keeping you in defeat. You will embark on an upward cycle of lasting transformation!

CHAPTER 3

1. "And why worry about your clothing? Look at the lilies of the field and how they grow. They don't work or make their clothing, yet Solomon in all his glory was not dressed as beautifully as they are. And if God cares so wonderfully for wildflowers that are here today and thrown into the fire tomorrow, he will certainly care for you" (Matt. 6:28–30 NLT). These words of compassion from Jesus suddenly rekindled embers of hope in the man.

2. The man with leprosy heard that God actually cared for and about him. For the first time in years, he wondered, *Is this possible? That God wants to be a Father to me? A heavenly Father Who would clothe me much better than the lilies, which are better clothed than Solomon in all his glory, if I put my trust in Him? Is it possible that God is reaching out to me with kindness, acceptance, and love, and inviting me to taste and receive His goodness?*

3. Galvanized by the hope inspired by the unmistakable compassion in Jesus' voice, the man crawled out of his makeshift shelter the moment Jesus finished speaking. All thoughts of staying hidden were gone. All he wanted to do was to go to Jesus and ask Him to take his disease away.

4. Jesus was already coming straight toward him. Instead of having gone straight down to the crowds after preaching to them, the Lord had turned another way to go toward the lone, afflicted man, as if He already knew all about the man's need and where he was.

5. Without hesitation, Jesus reached out and touched him. "I am willing," He said. "Be cleansed." And in that moment, from head to toe, smooth, unblemished skin covered the man's fully restored body. He was cleansed! The power of Jesus had, in an instant, swallowed up his uncleanness and given him his life back!

6. Romans 10:17 (NASB) says, "So faith comes from hearing, and hearing by the word of Christ." Because the man with leprosy heard words of grace—how God wanted to be a loving Father to him and provide for all his needs—faith arose in his heart, giving him the confidence to approach the Lord Jesus for his miracle.

7. It can mean the difference between receiving your miracle and remaining where you are in your lack or bondage. It can draw you close to God, or drive you further away from Him.

Faith comes by hearing, but fear also comes by hearing. If you've been hearing about a God Who is mostly angry and out to get you for your sins, that He gives people (even believers) sicknesses and punishes them with horrible accidents for their sins, that He wants you and your family in poverty to keep you humble, how can you possibly trust God for anything good to happen to you?

8. Acts 10:38 tells us that Jesus "went about doing good and healing all who were oppressed by the devil, for God was with Him." That tells us that God wants to do good, not evil, to us!

9. Jesus said, "He who has seen Me has seen the Father" (John 14:9). He is God's will in action, and He went about doing *good*—saving, delivering, healing, restoring, providing, guiding, and loving the unlovable. That's our God! That is His heart toward you!

10. Keep hearing messages full of the grace and finished work of our Lord Jesus as was proclaimed by the apostle Paul. This will impart faith and hope to you (see Acts 14:7–9). Keep hearing about how your sins have all been forgiven through Christ and how you are today the righteousness of God in Christ. Keep hearing about how much God loves you and wants to be a loving Father to you, to watch over you, provide for you, and deliver you from all your fears and afflictions. When you know God's love for you, it will cause you to run to Him instead of hiding from Him. His love upon you and in you will make you strong and cause you to overcome every temptation and fear.

11. Calli said, "Legalistic teachings had led me to believe that my sin was greater than the grace of our Lord Jesus Christ and His finished work on the cross. As a result, I lived in constant fear that I would lose my salvation every time I sinned. My past haunted me and I could never seem to outrun it as the torment simply overwhelmed me."

12. Calli said that churches started developing "compassion fatigue" and got tired of praying for her. She was even told, "Perhaps your schizophrenia is your cross to bear." Feeling they had given up on her and that she was the "beaten leftovers of the church," she immersed herself deeper in her sinful lifestyle. The Lord's response to Calli was to remind her of His love, that she was His and that He had been upholding her and waiting for her to turn to Him and to hear His voice.

14. "The people who know their God shall be strong, and carry out great exploits."

15. Keep hearing and growing in your knowledge of God's grace and mercy toward you. In Daniel's story, the Lord, through an angel, addressed him as a "man greatly beloved" (Dan. 10:11). So the more you hear about and are confident in His love for you, the more you will live life with boldness and a different, excellent spirit that sets you apart from others and testifies of His power in your life.

16. David knew God as a covenant-keeping God Who loved him. David would have been reminded of God's love for him every time he heard his own name called, for David's name means "beloved," the beloved of the Lord. David became such an amazing person because he knew and was conscious of how much the Lord loved him. Even when David failed, it was his

revelation that he was still beloved of the Lord that kept him going.

17. The word "knowledge" here is the Greek *epignosis,* which refers to a heart experience of what and Who God is rather than mere intellectual knowledge of facts about Him. It is a knowledge that is gained through an intimate and personal relationship with God. In other words, when you hear and hear until you know *in your heart* that the Lord loves you and is for you, you will experience His unmerited favor and supernatural peace in the area of your challenges. That is when you will find His strength, wisdom, and supply multiplied tangibly in your life.

18. God said to Gideon, "The Lord is with you, you mighty man of valor! . . . Surely I will be with you, and you shall defeat the Midianites as one man" (Judg. 6:12, 16). When he began to see how the Lord saw him, and believed that the Lord was with him and for him, he fulfilled his destiny! When you keep hearing how because of Jesus' sacrifice and finished work, nothing can separate you from God's love. When you know who you are in Christ and believe in God's love for you, you will become strong and you will see God do great things in and through you.

CHAPTER 4

1. Raised under legalistic teaching, Joni said she always saw God as another authority figure in her life, Who loved to point out her mistakes.

2. Joni said, "I began repeating, 'I am righteous in Christ,' even though that was SO far from how I felt at that moment. As I continued reading, I started to see what Daddy God was all about—peace, love, faith, truth, and most of all, FORGIVENESS! I discovered that my sins were on that cross with His Son, so I could move on from all my failures. I did not have to drag them around anymore. . . . I am just resting in Christ! I don't have to work for Him to love me. I just crawl into His lap and let Him love me."

4. In Roman 4:7–8 (NLT), David said, "Oh, what joy for those whose disobedience is forgiven, whose sins are put out of sight. Yes, what joy for those whose record the Lord has cleared of sin."

5. It leads to all kinds of insecurities, fears, and destructive bondages. Fear and insecurity cannot exist in a healthy relationship with God. In a marriage relationship, for example, if a wife never feels secure in her husband's love for her, she will never draw strength from or find joy in her marriage. Instead of thriving, that marriage will disintegrate over time. Similarly, our heavenly Father does not want us to live trapped in perpetual insecurity because we are never sure of our forgiveness.

6. Of course not! While everyone's sin is paid for, to be saved, every individual needs to make a personal decision to receive the forgiveness of all their sins by receiving Jesus as their personal Lord and Savior. Jesus is the only way to salvation. There is no other way except

through Jesus and His shed blood and resurrection. To be saved, you have to confess with your mouth that Jesus is your Lord and believe in your heart that God raised Him from the dead.

7. It tells us that Christ is risen! And according to this Scripture, because He is risen, you are no longer in your sins. Jesus' resurrection is the living proof that all your sins have been completely and totally forgiven.

8. It is all by grace through faith.

9. You are made righteous in God's eyes when you believe or put your faith in Christ and His sacrifice for you. It is through Jesus' obedience that we have been made righteous and justified from all our sins. Justification is our Lord Jesus removing all the guilt and penalty of sin and proclaiming that we have been made righteous by His shed blood.

10. Believe and learn to declare that you are saved, forgiven, made righteous (justified) by grace through faith in Christ. You'll see His favor, wisdom, power, and every benefit of His finished work released into your situation to turn everything around for His glory.

11. The verb for "have" is in the Greek present tense, which indicates durative action, meaning we are continually having forgiveness of sins, including every sin we will ever commit.

12. The Greek perfect tense is used here for "are forgiven," meaning this forgiveness is a definite action completed in the past with the effect of this action continuing into the present. This means that God's forgiveness avails for you in your present, and continues into your future.

13. The word "all" is the Greek *pas,* meaning "every kind or variety . . . the totality of the persons or things referred to." It refers to "all, any, every, the whole." So "all" means *all.* God's forgiveness of our sins covers *every* sin—past, present, and future! When we received the Lord Jesus as our Savior, we received the total and complete forgiveness of all our sins.

14. *Merriam-Webster Online* describes *sanctification* as "the state of growing in divine grace as a result of Christian commitment after conversion." *Sanctification* is an ongoing process in your growth as a Christian. This means that the more you grow in your relationship with the Lord Jesus, the more holy you will become in every area of your life.

15. We see in the Scriptures the apostle Paul telling Timothy to be "strong in the grace that is in Christ Jesus" (2 Tim. 2:1). The apostle Peter also encouraged believers to build a strong foundation with these closing words in his last epistle: "Grow in the grace and knowledge of our Lord and Savior Jesus Christ" (2 Pet. 3:18). This happens when you hear preaching and teaching that unveils the person of Jesus and His finished work.

CHAPTER 5

1. She longed for a deeper, fuller experience with Jesus, one in which she could have continuous enjoyment of abundant life. Most of all, she wanted to be able to trust Jesus fully for complete forgiveness of sins, enjoy intimacy with God, and have a rock-solid assurance of her salvation.

2. Frances understood that the Greek word for "cleanses" in 1 John 1:7 is in the present tense, which means that Jesus' blood shed two thousand years ago *continually cleanses or keeps on cleansing*. She said, "It was that one word 'cleanseth' which *opened the door of a very glory of hope and joy to me*. I had never seen the force of the tense before, a continual present, always a present tense, not a present which the next moment becomes a past. It goes on cleansing, and I have no words to tell how my heart rejoices in it. Not a coming to be cleansed in the fountain only, but a remaining in the fountain, so that it may and can go on cleansing."

3. Frances' revelation of the ever-cleansing blood of Jesus ushered in the richness of God's perfect peace into her heart and mind that is described in Isaiah 26:3. Resting in God's peace, she found ever-increasing and deepening victory, blessings, freedom from worry, and confidence that no matter what life brought her, she was abiding in God's love.

4. Because Jesus' blood continually cleanses you, you don't have a sometimes-yes-sometimes-no salvation, but a salvation that has secured a *yes* to all of God's promises because of the blood of Jesus (see 2 Cor. 1:19–20)!

5. The book of *Hebrews* was written to the Hebrews, or Jewish people (which included believers as well as nonbelievers). Hebrews 10:26–29, in particular, is addressing Jewish brethren who had received "the *knowledge* of the truth" (the Lord Jesus as their Messiah and His finished work), but never received this truth *into their hearts.* They heard the truth about Jesus, but were still going back to the temple to offer animal sacrifices for their sins. This was an insult to the Spirit of grace, because they were flatly rejecting the Lord Jesus, Who in His great grace had offered Himself as the perfect and final sacrifice for their sins at Calvary.

6. It is to commit the *specific sin* of knowing the truth that Jesus is the final sacrifice, and yet choosing not to accept His finished work.

7. Simply because genuine believers have already believed in Jesus' sacrifice and put their trust in the Lord's finished work, and they are certainly not going back to any temple to offer animal sacrifices for sin.

8. This judgment applies to unbelievers who hear the truth of the gospel of grace, and with open eyes turn their backs on our Lord Jesus and the salvation He offers. That is what it means to sin willfully today and insult the Spirit of grace. As long as a person keeps rejecting Jesus' perfect sacrifice and finished work, there no longer remains a sacrifice for his sin. He has rejected the only sacrifice God accepts. In the end, this unbeliever will have to face judgment for his rejection of the Lord. Having said this, the Bible makes it clear that God's heart is

not in punishment or judgment. Instead, He is "compassionate and gracious, slow to anger and abounding in lovingkindness" (Ps. 103:8 NASB). This is why God sent His Son—so that whoever believes in Him shall not perish (John 3:16).

9. Jesus said in John 5:24, "Most assuredly, I say to you, he who hears My word and believes in Him who sent Me has everlasting life, and shall not come into judgment [*krisis*], but has passed from death into life." The same word for "judgment" (*krisis*) used in Hebrews 10:27 is used here in this Scripture regarding believers. God wants believers to be assured that we will *never* come into *krisis* judgment! We have passed from death into life, as all of the fire of judgment fell fully on our Lord at Calvary.

10. If believers must confess their sin every time they sin, then every sin needs to be recognized and confessed (otherwise based on that verse, one is still unrighteous). It is humanly impossible to confess *every* sin, whether in thought, word, or deed. The constant, unceasing confession of one's sins makes the person extremely sin-conscious. The enemy takes advantage of what can become an obsession to confess every sin and places the person under constant condemnation. Some believers end up feeling they have lost their salvation because of their imperfect confession of sins.

11. John was not talking about confessing our sins every time we sin in thought or in deed. He was speaking of the need to acknowledge and confess to God that we are sinners because of Adam's sin, as well as to receive the total forgiveness for all our sins through Jesus' finished work.

12. Only once.

13. He reminds us that when we fail as believers, we have an Advocate with the Father— Jesus Christ. Because of our Lord Jesus and what He has accomplished at the cross, we have forgiveness and we still stand righteous before God even when we've missed it. As the apostle Paul reminded the Corinthian believers who had failed that they were still the temple of the Holy Spirit, John reminds us of who we are in Christ and Who we have representing us at God's right hand.

14. No, we confess our sins knowing that all our sins are *already* forgiven.

15. Because we have a close relationship with our heavenly Father, we can be honest with Him when we've done wrong. We can talk to Him about it, receive His grace for our weakness, and move forward knowing full well that He has already forgiven us through His Son's sacrifice. And we no longer worry about the fact that we can't possibly confess every sin, because we know it's not our confessions that save us, but the blood of Jesus. It results in a world of difference to our peace of mind!

CHAPTER 6

1. The curse of poverty is destroyed, broken hearts are mended, prisoners and the oppressed are set free, and the sightless receive sight! Through the preaching of God's amazing grace, people are set free to live a glorious and victorious life, not a life entangled with sin, doubt, apprehension, and defeat.

2. Truth is on the side of *grace*, not the Ten Commandments. In the original Greek text, the words for "grace" and "truth" are followed by a singular Greek verb for "came," which means that "grace" and "truth" are regarded as one item. Grace is the *truth* and this truth that sets people free is *grace*! So you cannot separate grace and truth—they are a composite whole.

3. Because grace, not the law, is the truth that sets you free and transforms you (see John 8:32).

4. Grace does not condemn the sinner but it also does not condone the sin. Grace, in the Person of Jesus, bore all of our sins at the cross so that God the Father can justly pardon the undeserving sinner. The result of such grace received is the power to go and sin no more. Isn't that beautiful? That's Who our Lord Jesus is. He loves the sinner and releases him or her with the power and strength to go and sin no more.

6. The first step to victory is to realize and believe that because the Lord Jesus has already taken the punishment for all your sins at the cross, you don't have to be bound and driven by guilt, condemnation, or fear. Every failure of yours has already been punished in Jesus' body and *you have perpetual forgiveness* and intimacy with God through Christ's blood! This is the power of right believing in the gospel that will lead you to experiencing inside-out transformation and lasting breakthroughs.

7. Because sin cannot take root in you when you are full of the consciousness of your right standing in Christ. The more you are established in God's gift of righteousness, the more you will walk in victory over sin and addiction. The Bible says, "Awake to righteousness and sin not" (1 Cor. 15:34). It is this awakening, in which you freely receive God's abundant grace and gift of righteousness, that empowers you to reign over sin!

8. Neil said, "I got a fresh revelation of who I am in Christ—I am the righteousness of God in Christ Jesus—and how there is no condemnation for those who are in Christ Jesus. . . . that I am perfect and holy in God's sight."

9. Neil says, "I remind myself that I am the righteousness of God in Christ, and the temptation loses any hold on me."

11. No, "salvation" is the ultra-rich Greek word *soteria,* which means "deliverance, preservation, safety, salvation." It covers any area of your life that needs saving so that you can enjoy wholeness and well-being in your body, soul, and spirit.

12. The gospel is so powerful because in it is the revelation that you have been made righteous by the work of Christ, not by your works. The good news is that when God looks

at a man who has put his faith in what Jesus has done, God sees him perfect, complete, and righteous in Christ. It is knowing this and growing in this revelation that unleashes the power and salvation of God in all its richness into all areas of our lives.

CHAPTER 7

1. Proverbs 18:10 tells us, "The name of the LORD is a strong tower; the righteous run to it and are safe." Don't put your trust in your own understanding. Instead, lean wholly on the one Who is more interested in your success than you are. Run to Him and cast all your cares upon Him for He cares for you (see 1 Pet. 5:7).

2. In the new covenant of grace, your righteousness is from the Lord Jesus Himself. Now, the more you understand your righteousness in Christ, the more you will experience His promise in Isaiah 54:17.

3. God's Word proclaims that none of these weapons, even if they have already been formed, shall prevail against you. And every unfounded accusation, every malicious lie, and every false allegation you shall condemn! The enemy doesn't have a hold over your life. God does, and He upholds all things in your life (see Heb. 1:3)!

4. We can't inherit the promised land based on our efforts to be justified through keeping perfectly the Ten Commandments. We can inherit it only through faith in the grace of our Lord Jesus. It is not by our works that we inherit God's promises, but by Christ's perfect, finished work.

5. The ram's horn is a beautiful picture of the death of our Lord Jesus. The ram had to die for the horn to be obtained. The sounding of the ram's horn is thus a proclamation of our Lord's death and finished work. At the cross, when Jesus had paid fully for all our sins with His blood, He proclaimed, "It is finished!" (John 19:30).

6. The lambs' blood typifies the shed blood of Jesus, the true Lamb of God, applied to our hearts, which brings us out of captivity and into the promised land. It is all Christ and Christ alone!

7. The message is that you are saved by grace through faith, but then in the same breath, this message goes on to corrupt the simplicity of the gospel by saying that you stay saved or get blessed through works. You'll also hear about all sorts of things that you need to do for God in order to be qualified through right living.

9. "Justified." She says, "I finally understood, without a doubt, that I am justified by the blood of the Lamb of God, Christ—even though I am still not perfect in my conduct!"

10. Bible reading has been a joy, healing has come, being blessed to be in the right place at the right time to experience miracles, and being lifted out of deep depression and despair onto a path of joy, peace, and hope.

11. The irony is that in trying to keep God's laws to be righteous, people produce works of

the flesh, such as adultery, fornication, hatred, heresies, and drunkenness (see Gal. 5:18–21). Why? Because "the strength of sin is the law" (1 Cor. 15:56). The law arouses or stirs up the sinful passions within our flesh (see Rom. 7:5).

12. In the first four chapters, Paul talks about grace, contrasting it with the law and contending earnestly for justification by faith, because the Galatian Christians were going back under the law. Paul was essentially bringing them back under *pure grace*, before talking to them about the fruit of the Spirit.

13. True holiness/right living comes when you keep hearing, receiving, and are conscious of your righteousness by grace through faith in Christ. Paul contrasts the *works* of the flesh and the *fruit* of the Spirit. Works are a result of *self-effort* that comes from being under the heavy demands of the law. *Fruit* is a result of life! Just as a tree will naturally produce good fruit when it is well watered and receiving the right amount of sunlight, so a Christian will produce good fruit without self-effort when he or she is well watered by the word of His grace and exposed to the sunshine of God's love.

CHAPTER 8

1. Jesus knew it was exactly what this poor man needed to hear for his healing to manifest. And indeed, at Jesus' next words, "Stand up, pick up your mat, and go to home," the paralyzed man "jumped up, grabbed his mat, and walked out through the stunned onlookers" (Mark 2:11–12 NLT). What had transpired? Jesus saw, when no one else could, that the man needed to hear he was forgiven, that God was not condemning him. And those words opened the door to his healing and broke him loose from his paralysis.

2. The assurance that beyond any doubt God is not withholding your breakthrough from you. He loves you, understands your pain and suffering, and has forgiven you through the cross. He wants you to know that your past does not have to poison your future. No matter how many dark days you have experienced, God has prepared many wonderful open doors of opportunity, favor, and good success for you to walk through in the days ahead.

3. The gift of forgiveness, of no condemnation, of righteousness, of eternal life, and the different gifts of the Spirit that God has placed in all our lives!

4. When we received Jesus as our Lord and Savior, we were so perfectly cleansed by the blood of Jesus—once and for all—that the Holy Spirit now lives *in* us and abides with us *forever* (see John 14:16–17)!

5. It means that God identified us as His own by giving us the Holy Spirit. The Holy Spirit is God's guarantee that He will give us the inheritance He has promised and that He has purchased us to be His own people. God sealed you with the Holy Spirit of promise to attest that you have been given the free gift of righteousness and the gift of eternal life through Jesus' finished work.

6. Pete said, "I felt like I was born again, all over again!" Since he understood that all of his sins are forgiven, his faith has shot through the ceiling and his life has been radically transformed! And this truth has born fruit in his wife and four kids as well.

7. Daphne said, "This self-condemnation and the belief that we are never going to be able to do what God expects of us often sends us back to drink, develop an addiction to drugs, and even die as a result of complications."

8. Daphne heard about God's grace. Grace and truth in the person of Jesus came and made all the difference. Change happened in her when she understood and believed that everything had already been done for her at the cross, and that Jesus wanted to heal her and pour His grace into her life because He loves her.

9. The only answer is an unshakable revelation of what happened at the cross and of your righteous identity in Christ. At the cross Jesus took your place of punishment and condemnation and became the full payment for all your sins. And when you believed in Jesus, you were justified by faith! The cross of Calvary has made all the difference.

10. A revelation of the grace of God. You need to study, meditate upon, and feed on the gospel of grace. Be strong in the grace of God extended to you. Be strong in understanding that your sins are forgiven. Be strong in the knowledge that you are justified by faith through grace. Be strong in the revelation that today, you are the righteousness of God in Christ.

11. When you are strong in the gospel of grace, you will produce a godly, holy, and glorious life! In the same way that you can't touch water and not become wet, you can't "touch" grace and not become holy. And this holiness is a true holiness that comes from the inside out. It is a holiness that flows from a grateful heart that has been emancipated from self-condemnation. We are not talking about superficial outward changes. We are talking about changes that happen in the deepest recesses of a person's heart, motivations, and thoughts.

12. It brought lasting freedom from alcoholism and self-condemnation as well as produced in her a desire to help other precious ladies who are struggling with alcoholism and condemnation. She doesn't *have* to volunteer her time to help these women, but she *wants* to. That's what grace does in a person's life. It transforms the person from the inside out. Grace makes a person gracious, kind, and generous. The gift of righteousness in you will produce fruits of righteousness.

13. People can't see with their physical eyes that you have been justified by faith. You may tell your friends that God has made you righteous, but they are not necessarily going to believe you or give weight to your words until they see your good works or a positive change in your behavior. They condemn or justify you based on what you do.

14. The truth is that once a person has been born again, it may not happen right away, but the grace that God has placed in him will one day produce good fruit in his life (see Rom. 2:4). That forgiveness and love experienced will overflow to others (see 1 John 4:19 NLT). Grace is the cause; good works are the effect. Focus on the cause and the effects will eventually come.

15. When you're discouraged by your failures, Jesus reassures you in Matthew 12:20 that God is not going to break you or snuff you out and throw you aside. No, He will not give up on you. He will love you back into wholeness so that there is a song in your heart once more. He will reignite your passion to live for Him and His glory as you see His love for you. Keep coming back to the gospel truths of His grace. Be patient and give yourself time to grow in grace through the knowledge of our Lord Jesus (see 2 Pet. 1:2).

CHAPTER 9

1. First John 4:18 says, "There is no fear in love; but perfect love casts out fear, because fear involves torment." There is no fear in God's love. When you experience His perfect love, it will drive out all fears.

2. This verse proclaims that God SO loves you. And if you only knew how much He esteems and treasures His beloved Son, you would catch a glimpse of how much He loves you, because He gave up His Son—heaven's best and the delight of His heart—for you. The gospel of grace is all about unveiling God's perfect love—a love whose length and depth and height were demonstrated at the cross. A love that gave up the Son of God as your sin-sacrifice. A love that bore your sins and mine, so that we can receive His everlasting life and live free of any bondage.

4. Our God is love! He is slow to anger, gracious, and patient. He is full of forgiveness, lovingkindness, and tender mercies.

5. Jesus was never provoked and angry with sinners, prostitutes, or tax collectors. He did not berate the woman at the well who had five husbands, or the woman who was caught in adultery. He reserved His harshest words for the self-righteous, hard-hearted, grace-resisting scribes and Pharisees, but He was always kind and loving toward the sinners and outcasts of society. That's the nature of your heavenly Father!

6. Grace doesn't shun the sinner; grace *pursues* the sinner. Grace doesn't picket against those who fall short; grace embraces them into wholeness and brings about real inward transformation for them. Grace does not condemn those struggling against sin; grace produces holiness in them.

7. Jesus invited Himself over to Zacchaeus's home, loved him, and showed him grace. Before the night was over, Zacchaeus said to Jesus, "Look, Lord, I give half of my goods to the poor; and if I have taken anything from anyone by false accusation, I restore fourfold" (Luke 19:8). That's the power of grace! Jesus gave Zacchaeus no commandments, no condemnation, no laws . . . just grace, grace, and more grace. And Zacchaeus's heart was forever transformed.

8. The Lord gave the rich young ruler the law to bring him to the end of himself by showing him one thing he was lacking. The very first commandment is, "You shall have no other gods before Me" (Exod. 20:3). Yet money was his god—he walked away sorrowful when the Lord

asked him to sell all that he had (see Luke 18:20–23). And, in contrast to Zacchaeus, there is no record that he gave even one nickel to the poor.

9. The law demands, and it results in fear, guilt, and sorrow. Grace supplies, and it produces generosity, holiness, and inward heart transformation.

10. They end up conscious of failing God and with a fearful expectation of His punishment and judgment. Every bad thing that happens to them reinforces that fear. Even when things are going well, they are fearful of losing God's blessings or protection because of a mistake they may have just made. The result? Insecurity, dread, anxiety, and all kinds of fears become constant companions that rob them of the joy of living, let alone living life with boldness and confidence.

11. The Ten Commandments minister death and condemnation because no man is able to keep God's perfect law. Failure to keep the law at any point brings you under its curse, condemns you, and hangs a death sentence over your head. In contrast, the covenant of grace "exceeds much more in glory" because it ministers the spirit of liberty and the gift of God's righteousness.

12. Jesus came to fulfill the law on our behalf (see Matt. 5:17). And the law was perfectly fulfilled at the cross when He cried out, "Finished!" (see John 19:30). He met the demands of the first covenant, which is the Mosaic covenant of the Ten Commandments, in order to put the second, which is the new covenant of God's grace, into effect (see Heb. 10:9–10 NLT)!

13. You become free from the ministry of condemnation and the death it ministers—guilt, insecurity, dread, anxieties, and all sorts of debilitating fears. Condemnation robs you of peace in your heart and of joy in your relationship with your Father. It robs you of faith and confidence in His love and ability to save you. But when you know and believe you are not under the ministry of condemnation but the ministry of righteousness, you can come freely before your heavenly Father and cast every concern on your heart to Him. You will not be constantly fearful that your failures will cause Him to punish you or withhold His blessings and protection from you, because you know that Jesus bore the punishment meant for you upon Himself at the cross.

14. When believers don't believe that all their sins have been punished and forgiven through the death of Jesus Christ at the cross, their consciences are never at rest. As a result, the wages of sin, which is death, continues to oppress them and keep them under bondage. This is why it is so important to be established in the revelation of your complete forgiveness in Christ.

15. It tells us that through His death, our Lord broke the power of death the devil had over us. Why did He do all this? To "release those who through fear of death were all their lifetime subject to bondage." Clearly, our Lord Jesus wants us free from the fear of death and from any bondage.

16. She simply began to understand the true nature of God, that He was not the source of but was the solution to her problem, and she had a personal revelation of His love and finished

work. She says, "Jesus has come into all the dark areas of my life to be with me, befriend me, and warm me with His presence. He shows me the love and forgiveness of God and restores my hope for the future!"

CHAPTER 10

1. Kirk kept hearing about God's glorious grace and the gift of righteousness. He said, "I began feeding on God's love for me. My life became more meaningful because I discovered that it is no longer I who live—Jesus is the One Who operates in me. The more I focus on His love for me, the more I fall in love with Him, and the more the Bible becomes a book about His love."

2. Kirk said, "Jesus turned the turmoil of my divorce into a breakthrough. I started experiencing life like never before as God kept showing up in my daily living, healing me, and fixing issues in my life—even issues that I had not asked Him to fix."

3. Kirk said, "I am walking with boldness, knowing I'm fully safe and sound in Jesus Christ and that He is always there for me. Eternal life is my inheritance in Christ Jesus by faith, not by my self-works."

4. Ask yourself: Does the teaching you are hearing cause you to want to live a life that glorifies our Lord Jesus? Does it emphasize your works or His work? Does it cause you to be occupied with yourself or occupied with our Lord Jesus?

5. This teaching does not exalt or glorify our Lord Jesus. You CANNOT talk about eternal salvation without the person of Jesus and His finished work at the cross. Jesus is the only way! Jesus said, "I am the way, the truth, and the life. No one comes to the Father except through Me" (John 14:6).

6. Correction in the new covenant takes place through His Word. Paul tells us, "All Scripture is inspired by God and profitable for teaching, for reproof, for correction, for training in righteousness" (see 2 Tim. 3:16 NASB). As mentioned in chapter 2, as you hear the Word preached, wrong beliefs and thinking begin to be replaced by right believing in God's grace, and change that brings about right living happens. Notice also how correction through God's Word includes "training in righteousness," which is believing right that you have been justified or made righteous by faith in our Lord Jesus. Oftentimes the Holy Spirit uses God-appointed leadership to accomplish this (see Gal. 6:1, 2 Tim. 4:2, 2 Thess. 3:15)—to point you back to Jesus' finished work and who you are in Christ. That is why it is so vital that you be a part of a local church with good leaders.

7. The apostle Paul corrected them by firmly reminding them of their righteous identity in Christ. He then goes on to remind them that their bodies are temples of the Holy Spirit. All this tells us that anyone who is reminded of and has a revelation of his or her righteousness in Christ will have the power to overcome sin!

8. From your being firmly rooted and established in the grace of God. You have the power to love, because He first loved you! The more you receive His love, the more you allow His love to flow through you. This is why the Bible declares that "love is the fulfillment of the law" (Rom. 13:10).

9. Whenever you have an unclean thought, or a stirring in you, or a temptation to sin, stop for a while and look to Jesus. See the cross. See and experience His love, forgiveness, and grace for you afresh. Know that He still loves you and is with you to strengthen you. Jesus is your victory over every temptation, addiction, and bondage!

10. The apostle Paul said, "For the good that I will to do, I do not do; but the evil I will not to do, that I practice" (Rom. 7:19). So the answer is not to depend on your willpower to say no to temptation, but to depend on God's grace and say yes to Jesus!

11. Your liberty from every sinful habit is found in the person of Jesus! He is your righteousness and holiness. To say yes to Jesus means to let Him come into the areas where you feel the weakest and allow His grace to transform you from the inside out.

CHAPTER 11

1. He is speaking "peace" to us, which is the Hebrew word *shalom,* meaning completeness, soundness, well-being in body and mind, safety, contentment, and peace in our relationships with people. This is His heart for us.

2. Focus on hearing Jesus and growing in the knowledge of Him and His grace. The Bible tells us that grace and peace (and every good blessing) are multiplied to us when we grow in the knowledge of Jesus our Lord (see 2 Pet. 1:2).

3. Peter didn't realize that by saying this, he was putting Jesus on the same level as Moses and Elijah.

4. His first words when His disciples were terrified were not words pertaining to a new law or commandment. They were words of grace. And in those words, you see the nature of our Lord. His presence and His words will always lift you up—spirit, soul, and body—when you are feeling down or in fear.

5. The message for believers is that Christ has replaced the law, and God wants us to always be hearing His Son's words of grace. The law of Moses has served its purpose to bring man to the end of himself. The prophets have also served their purpose of reminding man of God's laws. Both have served their purposes. Now it is the day of grace. It is the day of the Son of God—not the *servants* of God, but the *Son* of God Himself.

6. Keep hearing about how our Lord Jesus loved to heal and still heals today. Hear how He bore the cruel Roman lashes for you, so that by His stripes, you are healed (see Isa. 53:5). Hear how He went about doing good and healing ALL who were oppressed (physically, emotionally, and mentally) by the devil (see Acts 10:38, Matt. 9:35). Hear how when He saw the crowds

waiting for His healing touch, He was moved with compassion—He didn't see them as people with impossible demands, but as sheep without a shepherd (see Matt. 9:36). And hear how He is the same yesterday, today, and forever (see Heb. 13:8). Faith will infuse your spirit, and His divine healing and health will flood every cell, organ, and system of your body!

7. Keep hearing how God is for you and not against you. Hear how He has freely given you ALL things through Christ (see Rom. 8:31–32), so that all you need to do is to freely receive ALL of His blessings, including the favor, wisdom, healing, and supply you need for whatever challenge you may be facing. Hear the Son remind you of your loving heavenly Father, Who knows your every need and promises He will take care of you as you cast your cares on Him and simply seek first His gift of righteousness (see Matt. 6:31–33). As you listen and become established in His grace toward you, every worry and anxiety will evaporate like mist as the morning sun comes up, and you will see His fresh supply of favor for every new need.

8. Hear the Lord's words of affirmation to you, "I will never leave you nor forsake you." Let these words restore your heart, bring stability to your emotions, and give you the faith to boldly say, "The Lord is my helper; I will not fear. What can man do to me?" (Heb. 13:5–6).

9. Under the law of Moses, the temple tax was for the maintenance of the temple, which was built for God. Peter was still thinking of Moses and what Moses said about the temple tax. He didn't even ask or consult Jesus, even though he'd just been told to "hear Him."

10. James and John were listening to Elijah and looking to him as the example to follow. Jesus responded, "You do not know what manner of spirit you are of. The Son of Man is not come to destroy men's lives but to save them" (Luke 9:55–56). The spirit of Elijah is a spirit of judgment. Jesus told the two brothers very plainly that by saying what they did, they were not of the spirit of grace.

11. Because neither the law nor the prophets hold the answer to our deepest cry for intimacy and peace with God, and to enjoyment of His presence and power in every area of our lives.

12. Whereas Moses failed and Elijah became discouraged, the Scriptures tell us that our Lord Jesus, the altogether lovely One, "will not fail nor be discouraged" (Isa. 42:4). Whereas Moses was impatient, our Lord Jesus is patient with you and me today especially when we make mistakes and fail. And whereas Moses failed to bring God's people into the promised land, our Lord Jesus finished the work His Father sent Him to do and has ushered us into all of God's blessings and promises (see Eph. 1:3, 2 Cor. 1:20). Whereas Elijah became discouraged, Jesus was not discouraged even by people's repeated rejection of Him. He is your rock and your fortress when you are feeling discouraged.

CHAPTER 12

1. This statement reflects man's pride and self-confidence. This is not an indictment against the children of Israel, but against all men who boast they can keep all of God's laws. When people say that they can well keep God's laws even before they have heard what those laws are, that is putting confidence in the flesh. That is pride.

2. The Lord told Moses to set bounds for the people around Mount Sinai and to warn them not to go up to the mountain or touch its base or they would surely be put to death (see Exod. 19:12–13).

3. "Now all the people witnessed the thunderings, the lightning flashes, the sound of the trumpet, and the mountain smoking; and when the people saw it, they trembled and stood afar off. Then they said to Moses, 'You speak with us, and we will hear; but let not God speak with us, lest we die'" (Exod. 20:18–19).

4. Don't fall from grace by attempting to make yourself right with God by the law. When you do this, you cut yourself off from Christ and His grace, which is your supply for every need and challenge. Stop rejecting, fighting, and shoving away God's grace. Rather, allow His love, grace, and power to lift you up from every defeat you are experiencing.

5. Mount Sinai, the mountain of the law, only breeds fear and insecurity in your relationship with God and drives you deeper into destructive behaviors with no hope of freedom. Because of the cross of Jesus, where God's wrath for all our sins was poured out, He has moved to Mount Zion, the mountain of grace, the place of reconciliation, relationship, and closeness with His people. On this mountain you find intimacy with the Lord that gives you strength and changes you from the inside out.

6. It promises that Mount Zion cannot be removed. It remains forever! It means that if you establish your life on Mount Zion, you will enjoy true liberty and stability. If your blessings and breakthroughs come from Mount Zion, they will last!

7. It is only because of the sacrifice and finished work of His Son, Jesus. The Hebrew word for "Zion" is *Tsiyown,* which means "parched place." A parched place is a place that has been made dry or burned by intense heat. Mount Zion speaks of Mount Calvary, the place where Jesus, the sacrificial Lamb of God, was burned by God's fiery indignation against all our sins. Mount Zion typifies the finished work of our Lord Jesus at the cross. He was made sin so that we can be made righteous (see 2 Cor. 5:21).

9. *Goshen* literally means "drawing near" to God. In the midst of all the darkness and uncertainty you may see in the world today, know that there is a Goshen you and your family can take refuge in. It's a blessed place where God says, "You shall be *near* to me, you and your children, and your children's children. There *I will provide for you!*"

10. Out of that intimacy, barrenness gives way to fruitfulness. Lack is replaced by abundance. Sadness and sickness with joy and life. Fear with love. Confusion and insecurity with peace and assurance. Defeat with victory. Breakdowns with breakthroughs. And aimlessness with divine destiny!

12. You can be a prisoner of hope and receive God's gift of righteousness afresh to reign over it (see Zech. 9:12, Rom. 5:17). You can have a fresh start in your career even when you have seen your dreams shattered, because you know that in the place of nearness, God loves you, hears you, and will restore to you. You can live free of fear, terror, and oppression as you become more and more established in His righteousness day by day (see Isa. 54:14).

CHAPTER 13

1. Mary understood the value of our Lord implicitly. She didn't see Him as just a man, but as God in the flesh Who loved her and came to be her Savior. Because she esteemed Jesus so greatly, anointing Him with her most valuable possession was simply an outward representation of just how much she loved, valued, and cherished Him inwardly.

2. Judas was indignant and saw this as a waste because he couldn't see the value of Jesus. What Judas Iscariot saw as waste, Mary saw as worship. To her, the person of our Lord Jesus was priceless.

3. These people do not understand the value of our Lord Jesus, much like Judas.

4. Just ask yourself—how is our Lord Jesus valued in this teaching? Does it make you want to worship, praise, and glorify Him with your life? Or does it put more value on you and what you have to perform? Does it cause you to be centered on and occupied with the person of Jesus? Or does it cause you to be centered on and occupied with yourself and whether you have failed or succeeded?

5. These children come from families that are full of love and affirmation. Families that free them to succeed. These children are not afraid to fail and they stand out in the crowd because they dare to be different for the glory of our Lord Jesus Christ. They dare to say no to the influences of the world. They are not ashamed when their peers mock their Christian values.

6. In an environment full of love, grace, and affirmation, the child's parents are also able to discipline, correct, and guide the child in learning to make good decisions for himself without crushing his spirit.

7. We are highly favored and always loved by our Father in heaven as a result of our identity as the sons and daughters of God through the finished work of Jesus Christ. It is a matter of our identity, not our performance. It is based on *who* we are and *Whose* we are, not what we have or have not done. The more you value what Christ has done for you to make you a forgiven, righteous, and beloved child of God, the more you become established in your true identity in Christ.

8. When we know that our heavenly Father loves us, we can receive correction and discipline with gratefulness and humility. That is why it is so important for every child of God to experience the grace revolution—to become established in His perfect love and anchored in His unconditional grace toward them. Grace imparts to us the power to live a whole and victorious life—to overcome sin, love others, and live a life above defeat. Grace is the key to holiness.

9. They live in perpetual guilt and condemnation, punishing themselves and subjecting themselves to self-destructive behavior. They don't know all that our Lord Jesus has sacrificed on the cross for their forgiveness, deliverance, redemption, and freedom.

10. Many become bound to alcohol, drugs, and all kinds of debilitating substance abuse. They often end up living in a state of constant fear and sleeplessness, and suffering psychosomatic illnesses and anxiety attacks.

11. You can stop punishing yourself today by receiving the truth that Jesus took all your punishment when He stood in your place at the cross. Our Lord was punished on the cross, so that today, you can be healed and made completely whole, body, soul, and spirit! Value our Lord Jesus and all that He has sacrificed on the cross for your forgiveness, your deliverance, your redemption, and your freedom!

12. Garrett had a stunning encounter with Jesus and His amazing grace. He said, "I had no idea that God could love a person like me after all I had done. I am now free! Free to be loved by God because of the finished work of our Lord Jesus Christ. I am free to hope, free to receive, and free to come to Jesus even when I fail."

14. In order to be a chief priest or a Pharisee, one needed to be a student of the Word of God from a young age, and to know the Torah from front to back. Yet the religious leaders, who were zealous for the law and knew all about the Torah, were the very people who plotted to kill Jesus. They had *head* knowledge but they did not have a heart for the person of Jesus. They had all this Bible knowledge, but they did not have the Author of the Bible in their hearts. They would constantly quote from the Old Testament to condemn and to crush those who have failed instead of saving them.

15. It is possible to accumulate a lot of head knowledge on *this* theology and *that* theology, and yet not have any heart knowledge that burns with love and passion for our Lord Jesus Christ. It is possible to enrich your mind or to study about this interpretation and that interpretation of the Scriptures, and still have a heart that is stone-cold when it comes to an intimate and personal relationship with Jesus.

16. We need to study the Bible not simply to accumulate head knowledge, but to have a revelation of the person of Jesus. To have a heart of love for Jesus, you need to get into the Word and know the Bible. True scriptural knowledge about Jesus will lead you to have a heart for Him.

17. It means you read the Word to feed on His beauty, His grace, His majesty, and His immense and sacrificial love for you. He is the bread of life and the more you feed on Him in the Word, the more you will be strengthened and nourished with His health, life, and wisdom for every area of your life. When you see Jesus in the Word, you will know how to esteem and value Him. Jesus becomes real food for your soul and He gives you strength for every area of your life.

18. Whatever you do for Jesus out of love for Him cannot be hidden. People will smell it. You will carry the fragrance of Christ all about you, and it's a fragrance of victory, not defeat! And whatever you give to Jesus is never forgotten. What you hold in your hand may be temporal. But the moment you put it into Jesus' hands, it becomes eternal.

19. Jesus did not only receive her worship, He enveloped her forever in the sweet incense of His praise of her. Today, we are still talking about and honoring what Mary did for our Lord two thousand years ago. When you worship Him out of an implicit value of His person, as Mary did, He'll cause your good works to have a lasting effect for generations to come!

20. In terms of value to God, whether it was a bullock, lamb, or pair of turtledoves, they were all equal and acceptable to Him, because they all pointed to the one final and perfect sacrifice of His beloved Son.

21. Many believers have a lamb-size revelation of Jesus. They know that Jesus is the Lamb of God Who has washed away their past sins with His blood. Then there are some Christians who have only a pigeon-size revelation of Jesus. They see Him as the Son of God Who came down from heaven to die for man's sins. And finally there are believers who have a bullock-size revelation of Jesus and His cleansing blood. As the bullock was the most valuable of the three sacrifices, it is a picture of believers today who are spiritually rich because they have a large and deep revelation of Jesus, His blood, and how it has cleansed them of all their sins.

22. Because everything starts from the inside out. That inward spiritual wealth (that comes from a revelation of the Lord's love and what He has accomplished for you) will translate into outward benefits of peace, stability, joy, provision, and victory. Back then, the wealthier you were, the bigger the size of your offering. Today, the larger your revelation of Jesus and His

finished work, the more spiritually wealthy you are. This is so much more valuable than having just material wealth.

CHAPTER 14

1. Notice that the verse is talking about a dog, not to a sheep (which refers to believers). There is no inward transformation that came from the power of God's grace. In the same way it is a sow (not a sheep) wallowing in the mire. Hence 2 Peter 2:22 refers to people who have never had a born-again experience of receiving Jesus as their Lord and Savior. In other words, they are *professors* and not *possessors* of Christianity.

2. The old is passed and the new has come. He is no longer a dog or sow, but a new creation in Christ Jesus. A sheep can fall and fail, but it will never want to wallow in vomit and mud. Sin—like vomit and mud—is contrary to the new nature a new creation has in Christ. True believers in Christ look for freedom *from* sin. They genuinely hate being entangled and bound in sin (see Rom. 6:14).

3. No, please notice that our Lord Jesus said to these people, "I *never knew* you" (emphasis mine). Now, how can this be applied to believers who have been born again and who have a relationship with the Lord? It is clearly referring to people who had never had a personal relationship with the Lord. This passage is to be used as a warning only against professors of the Christian faith, not against those who have genuinely accepted Jesus as their Lord.

4. So that you will be established in our Lord Jesus, and not be easily swayed and tossed and turned by every wind of doctrine (see Eph. 4:14). You are His precious child and your heavenly Father wants you to have a strong foundation built on your secure salvation in Christ.

5. The word "never" here is translated from the Greek particle *ou me,* which is a double negative, strongly emphasizing the meaning of "never, certainly not, not at all, by no means." In other words, once you are saved, you will never, by no means, ever perish!

6. Because grace isn't a teaching, doctrine, or formula. Grace is a person and His name is Jesus! Once you see our Lord Jesus as a person, once you see all His beauty, glory, grace, love, and forgiveness and begin to have a genuine relationship with Him, there is no way you would want to live a lifestyle that does not glorify His holy name. When you value Jesus in your life, you value His glory.

7. As we behold the person of Jesus and live under His grace, His grace teaches us to deny ungodliness and worldly lusts. As a result, we become people zealous for the glory of God in our lives and "zealous for good works."

8. The word "accepted" in 2 Corinthians 5:9 is not the Greek word *charitoo*. It is another Greek word, *euarestos,* which means "well pleasing." Hence the New King James translation says, "Therefore we make it our aim . . . to be well pleasing to Him."

9. *Euarestos* is not about your position in Christ. *Euarestos* refers to something that you do that brings your Father in heaven great delight and joy. In Christ the Beloved, we are already highly favored, but there are things that we can do to glorify and be extra pleasing to our Father in heaven.

10. Children are always highly favored in their parents' hearts. There is nothing they can ever do to change that position. It is a position anchored on their identity as their parents' children. Yet there are times when they do something special for their parents that brings great delight. In those moments, not only are they highly favored, they are also extra well pleasing to their parents. Do they have to do those special things to earn their parents' love? Absolutely not! They are already loved and highly favored. In fact, their desire to do something special for their parents stems from their having confidence in their parents' love for them. They desire to please their parents because they know just how much they already love them.

11. Paul said, "But by the grace of God I am what I am, and His grace toward me was not in vain; but I labored more abundantly than they all, yet not I, but the grace of God which was with me." He attributed all his ministry success to God's grace in his life.

12. When Jayden discovered and believed right about God's grace for him, he went from feeling defeated, condemned, and guilty about his failures to being Jesus-conscious, joyful, healed, and an unstoppable evangelist of the goodness and grace of God.

CHAPTER 15

2. People who have been touched by the grace of God are carriers of His Spirit of humility and graciousness. We are not people who render evil for evil, reviling for reviling. We are people called to be a blessing everywhere we go. That's the grace revolution in action.

3. Every time you speak well of something, you are blessing that thing and being a blessing!

4. Speak well of your marriage, your children, your family, and your friends. That's how you bless and become a blessing everywhere you go. Bless your body too, by speaking well of it—don't keep saying it's getting old! Speak well also of your relationship with the Lord. Call yourself the beloved of the Lord. Declare His protection, favor, and righteousness over you and your loved ones and begin to experience His blessings like never before.

5. Many times people don't realize that they are unintentionally cursing themselves and the people around them with the constant flow of negative words that they speak about themselves and others. Words of defeat, anger, bitterness, and complaint are toxic.

7. When our Lord spoke to the fig tree, it first dried up at its very roots before death reached the leaves. So don't be discouraged when you speak to your challenge and nothing seems to be happening. Believe that you are speaking directly to the root of the problem and that the outward manifestation of your faith is on its way!

8. She was standing on what Scripture says about the blood of Jesus. Exodus 12:13 says, "And when I see the blood, I will pass over you; and the plague shall not be on you to destroy you when I strike the land of Egypt." The presence of blood means that there has already been a death. It signifies that a payment has already been made. Today we can stand upon the unshakable foundation of God's promises because the Lamb of God was sacrificed at Calvary and His blood is on the doorposts of our lives.

9. The new covenant is all about right *believing,* whereas the old covenant is all about right *doing.* The new covenant is all about the power of *speaking* well, whereas the old covenant was about the power of *working* well. When a person believes right, he will live right. When a person believes that he is made righteous by the blood of Jesus Christ, he will be inwardly transformed to live right and the spirit of godliness will be evident in his life.

10. Notice that the word of faith is first in your mouth, and then it drops into your heart. When you speak words of faith, what you speak will finally drop into your heart, and what is in your heart will lead you. So when you are sick, speak well over yourself, declaring, "Lord Jesus, I thank You that by Your stripes I am healed."

11. The focus of the righteousness that is by the law is on *doing.* The focus of the righteousness of faith is on *speaking.*

12. In each case, the Lord did not speak what He saw, but He quickened the dead and brought non-existent things into existence with His spoken words!

13. Holding on to negative emotions will eat away at you on the inside. Holding bitterness against someone, for example, is like drinking lethal poison, and expecting the other person to die! It is just not worth it. You are killing yourself slowly.

14. Forgiveness is for those who don't deserve it. That's what grace is all about. Remember what the Word says: don't return evil for evil, reviling for reviling. Instead, have a spirit of grace and bless those who curse you. Choose life and let go of that anger in your heart. Release that person, and most importantly, release yourself. Bless them and set yourself free to love life and see many good days.

15. Love life and see good days. Start by refraining your lips from speaking evil and begin filling your mouth with the good news of all the wonderful things our Lord has done and will continue to do in your life.

CHAPTER 16

1. Many believers who are struggling with sin, addictions, and destructive bondages don't have the revelation of their new covenant identity in Christ. When you see a believer struggling with sin, it is often a case of mistaken identity.

2. Paul told the Corinthians who had fallen into sin, "Know ye not that your bodies are the members of Christ? . . . know ye not that your body is the temple of the Holy Ghost which is in you, which ye have of God, and ye are not your own? For ye are bought with a price: therefore glorify God in your body, and in your spirit, which are God's" (1 Cor. 6:15, 19–20 KJV). Paul knew that if they were reminded of their righteous identity in Christ, they would repent. They would return to grace and turn away from their sins when they were reminded of their value that is according to the heavy price that Christ had paid on the cross to ransom them.

3. The best way to help them is to point them back to their identity in Christ. They probably do not know, or have forgotten, how they have been made the righteousness of God through Jesus' blood.

4. Melissa said, "I didn't think of going to God and church because people I knew told me, 'You're going to go to hell because of your choices and how you're living. God's angry with you. He's disgusted with you.' This was what I believed about God, and thought there was no way I could come to Him."

5. She said she "discovered how God gave His best—His Son, Jesus—for me, so that I could have a relationship with Him as my Daddy God and come into His presence without fear or shame."

6. Melissa said that as she confessed her righteousness in Christ, "Amazingly, the temptations that held me in the past have all lost their hold. It feels like I'd never lived a destructive lifestyle. Today, my life testifies that Daddy God loves and saves. More importantly, the change has been effortless—it's all by the grace of Jesus. It's had nothing to do with my willpower but the divine power of Christ at work in me."

7. Like Melissa, they hear about an angry and capricious God who is just looking for an opportunity to club them with a big stick and send them to an eternal furnace of fiery damnation for their bad lifestyle choices, that God is disgusted and angry with them, and that He will never bless them.

8. All that those who are struggling with sinful lifestyles hear is, "WE HATE THE SIN," and they stay away from the church because they understandably equate that with "WE HATE YOU." That is simply not the gospel.

9. Our Lord never endorsed people's sinful lifestyles; He simply awakened them to His deep and personal love for them, and once they experienced His love, they had the power to walk out of the prison of sin, addiction, and bondage. The religious actively shunned the

sinner; Jesus actively pursued the sinner. Grace working in our lives does the same toward others, while setting us free from our own prisons.

10. Because after some time, they forget the scriptural revelation they received that gave them the breakthrough in the first place. Revelations can be stolen and forgotten. That's what happened to the Corinthian church and Paul had to step in to remind them of their righteous identity in Christ.

11. It is so essential for you to be part of a local church because that's where you can keep on hearing messages that are full of the person of Jesus, and be surrounded with Christ-centered leaders and friends who will always point you back to the Lord. The grace revolution is not just about momentary breakthroughs; it is about experiencing lasting and permanent breakthroughs.

12. Begin to speak of your righteous identity in Christ! When you are discouraged, when things look dark, speak out, speak up, and speak without doubt. And I promise you that you will start living more stress-free, more fearlessly, more boldly, and more victoriously than ever before!

CHAPTER 17

1. Refrain your lips from speaking evil. Know that you belong to the Lord, who watches over you like a tender shepherd over His flock. Declare, "It is well, in Jesus' name." Many times, the simplest prayers (like this one) are the most powerful prayers.

2. The Bible tells us, "He who is in you is greater than he who is in the world" (1 John 4:4). We are *His*! We are not like sheep without a shepherd. All the blessings, promises, and protection that belong to the righteous "are Yes, and in Him Amen" (see 2 Cor. 1:20). We need only receive them by grace through faith. They are not received through our works, so no man can boast, but purely through faith in His unmerited favor (see Eph. 2:8–9).

3. When fear works its way into your heart and you begin to get anxious about the safety of your children, just claim this promise in God's Word and say, "Lord, I thank You that I am the righteousness of God in Christ, and You promised in Your Word that the seed of the righteous shall be delivered."

4. Mary sat at our Lord's feet and just pulled, drew, and received from her Savior. Martha, on the other hand, was consumed with duty, responsibility, serving, and doing. Martha was zealous about serving the Lord, but she forgot the person for whom it was all about. Mary looked beyond the exterior and saw a fullness in the Lord to draw from. Martha saw Him in the natural, as needing her ministry.

5. Martha was utterly consumed by her duty and missed the divine deity, the Lord Jesus Himself, Who was sitting right in her living room! Our Lord's response was: "Martha, Martha,

thou art careful and troubled about many things: *But one thing is needful*: and Mary hath chosen that good part, which shall not be taken away from her" (Luke 10:41–42 KJV, emphasis mine). He lovingly dealt with the root issue of what was troubling her heart (not her service to Him), and gave her a revelation of how she could, like her sister, learn to draw from Him.

6. Keep receiving from Jesus. Every day, receive His Word, His grace, and His gift of righteousness. And keep confessing your righteousness in Him—it will result in you doing the right thing at the right time as an overflow of an intimate relationship with the Lord.

7. This teaching argues that while all our sins are forgiven *judicially* because of the penalty that Jesus paid on our behalf on the cross, we are out of fellowship with God when we commit a sin—until we confess that sin to receive *parental* forgiveness. If you go by this teaching, you will always feel you are lacking in parental forgiveness, simply because there will always be sins (in thought or deed) you have not confessed. The bottom line is that you won't have full assurance of your forgiveness in Christ. You will always be sin-conscious and doubt your forgiveness, and both your conscience and the devil will exploit this.

8. The apostle Paul preached the forgiveness of sins with no apology, no qualifications, and no distinction between judicial and parental forgiveness. So be careful of these man-made distinctions that are not in God's Word. Forgiveness is forgiveness; there are no subdivisions. You are either forgiven or you are not, and how much you enjoy your forgiveness depends on what you believe about our Lord Jesus and what He has done on the cross.

9. Say by faith, "I am strong in the strength of the Lord. I can do all things through Christ who strengthens me" (see Phil. 4:13).

10. Say by faith, "By His stripes I am healed" (see 1 Pet. 2:24).

11. Say by faith, "My God provides for all my needs according to His riches in glory by Christ Jesus" (see Phil. 4:19).

12. Say by faith, "I am the righteousness of God in Christ Jesus" (see 2 Cor. 5:21). Declare and reinforce your righteous identity in Christ. Those who receive the gift of righteousness receive the power to reign over sin (see Rom. 5:17)!

13. Jimmy said, "Within a few weeks, those sinful habits began to cease on their own! I began to effortlessly see victory in this area, and I no longer concentrated on 'not sinning' but on Jesus' finished work! What willpower, self-discipline, techniques, and methods could not do, God's grace did! I am free and am a living testimony that the GRACE OF GOD IS THE KEY TO OVERCOMING SIN!"

CHAPTER 18

1. Under the law of Moses, the injurer has to repay the full value of whatever was lost, defrauded, or stolen plus one-fifth more to the party who suffered the loss. That amounts to 120 percent of the original value. How much more then can we expect restoration under the new covenant of grace—"a far better covenant with God, based on better promises" (Heb. 8:6 NLT). That means we can trust God for a 120 percent—and more—restoration!

2. The trespass offering is a picture of what Jesus did for us at the cross. He became our substitute and was judged in our place for every trespass we committed so that we can freely receive every blessing of God, including the blessing of restoration.

3. The most precious thing that our Lord Jesus can restore to you is the lost years of your life. All the years that the locusts have eaten, God can supernaturally restore to you. Every minute spent in fear, worry, doubt, guilt, condemnation, addiction, and sin adds up to wasted years that have been stolen from you. He is going to restore to you the years the locusts have eaten—and in greater measure than you can imagine. Your best days are ahead of you!

4. Clarence says that he found rest and freedom from condemnation, and that discovering God as his Dad meant all good things were his in Christ Jesus! He is running his own business, owns a home, and has had his relationship with his daughter restored. He says of what God has done: "Not only has He restored my life, but He has also restored my heart and mind toward Him."

6. Our Lord was speaking to the Jewish people, so "the truth" that they "*shall* know" could not have been the old covenant of the law, which they were already well versed in. Knowing and attempting to keep the law to earn their righteousness had not given them the freedom they sought. It had, in fact, become for them an impossibly heavy yoke to bear.

7. It was by faith (see Acts 15:9)! The Gentiles heard the forgiveness of sins being preached by Peter, *believed* the good news, and had their hearts *purified by faith.* Not by works, but by faith in Christ. Their hearts were purified by *believing right*—believing that those who believed in the Lord would receive the remission of sins and be made the righteousness of God. The same is true for us today!

8. According to the authority of God's Word, our hearts are purified *by faith* in our Lord Jesus. Hallelujah! Don't let people inject into your heart all kinds of beliefs that in order to have a pure heart and see the Lord's blessings in your life, you need to do this and that.

9. "Come to Me, all you who labor and are heavy laden, and I will give you rest. Take My yoke upon you and learn from Me, for I am gentle and lowly in heart, and you will find rest for your souls. For My yoke is easy and My burden is light" (Matt. 11:28–30).

10. The Lord Jesus says to you, "Come to Me, and I will give you *rest.*" Notice that the word "restoration" begins with "REST." So stop trying to be justified through the law of Moses. You are justified by faith. As you rest in His grace and finished work, you will receive your restoration!

11. Isaiah 61:2 says, "To proclaim the acceptable year of the LORD, *and the day of vengeance of our God*" (emphasis mine). Notice that Jesus didn't read past the comma about the day of God's vengeance. Why? Because our Lord, Who was standing in Nazareth as He read those Scriptures, had come to proclaim the acceptable year of our Lord—remember what He said next: "Today this Scripture is fulfilled in your hearing."

12. According to the Greek scholar Thayer, *dektos* is defined as "that most blessed time when salvation and the free favors of God profusely abound." Praise be to God, we are still in this *dektos* season. We are still in the acceptable year under the dispensation of grace and our preaching and understanding of God's Word must be according to this dispensation.

15. The result is a confusing theology. They preach grace and they also preach the law. They preach righteousness by faith, but they also preach righteousness by works. They preach that all your sins are forgiven, but then qualify that your sins aren't forgiven if you don't confess them. They take Scriptures that are specifically meant for Israel and apply them directly to the church today. They preach an unconditionally loving Father, but also an angry, frustrated, and disappointed God. What they think is "balance" is really mixture—and it results in confusion, fear, and doubt for all who hear them,

16. Valerie began to experience God's abundant restoration in quite literally every area of her life, beginning with an intimate relationship with Him, to restoration of physical health and blessed family relationships.

CHAPTER 19

2. Marcus said, "Even though I was in church, I wasn't sure God loved me or that He would heal me because I wasn't perfect. In fact, I was quite sure He would not heal me because I had messed up and hadn't done enough or made enough sacrifices to please Him. Some days, I was so depressed, I even wondered if God was real."

3. God wants His beloved children to live with great assurance of their salvation, forgiveness, and righteousness in Christ. And the Word of God, as we have seen repeatedly, imparts this full assurance of faith (for example, see 1 John 5:11–13).

4. It tells us that the Father's will was to send His only begotten Son to take away the first covenant, the covenant of law, and to establish the second covenant, the covenant of grace.

6. The Holy Spirit has been sent to *witness* to you that you have been made the righteousness of God in Christ. If you were standing in the courts of heaven, you would hear the Holy Spirit witnessing that your sins and lawless deeds are no more remembered by God.

7. Know that in God's grace and wisdom, He has placed us in a covenant where we cannot be made unrighteous. In the old covenant, there was no one who could be justified and made righteous by the law. But in the new covenant, all who believe in our Lord Jesus are made

eternally righteous. And we have the Holy Spirit to witness this powerful truth within us!

8. When you are led by the Holy Spirit today, He constantly reminds and assures you that you are righteous in Christ. The more you hear Him leading you in righteousness-consciousness, the more you will find Him leading you out of destructive habits, thoughts, relationships, and situations. He will remind you of your righteousness, even when you miss the mark and fail. In fact, *that's* the time you need the Holy Spirit's witness to pick you up from where you have fallen.

9. Instead of allowing you to sink deeper into the pit of sin, the Holy Spirit pulls you out of it. By the witness of the Holy Spirit, the righteous man knows he is still righteous in Christ. And because of that assurance, he will have the power to rise again.

10. Our Lord Jesus actually said that the Holy Spirit will "convict the *world* of sin." This noun *sin* is in the singular because it refers to the *one* sin of not believing in the Lord Jesus—"of sin, because they do not believe in Me." Before we became born-again believers, all of us responded to the Holy Spirit's conviction of the sin of unbelief in Christ and invited Jesus to be our Lord and Savior.

11. Jesus said that the Holy Spirit convicts us believers of our righteousness in Him—"of righteousness, because I go to My Father and you see Me no more [referring to his disciples which speak of all believers today]."

CHAPTER 20

1. The revelation that *the Lord is our righteousness* will cause God's people to fear no more, nor be discouraged, nor be in lack.

3. Just because you don't know the Bible from cover to cover, there is no reason to be intimidated by learned theologians. The gospel is so simple that even fishermen like Peter could grasp it, and yet it can also confound intellectual scholars such as Nicodemus. What is important is that we do not miss the forest for the trees and completely miss the entire point about the will of the Father, the work of the Son, and the witness of the Holy Spirit. Remember that the learned Nicodemuses of today might hear the gospel of grace preached and leave wondering, "How can these things be?"

4. Edwina said, "Pastor Prince shared how Jesus loved the woman caught in adultery unconditionally, giving her the gift of no condemnation to empower her to stop sinning. It was the first time I heard about a God who doesn't condemn me."

5. The Lord knows everything about you—every failure, every sin, and every shortcoming. But He still loves you with an everlasting love, a love that is completely unconditional, a love that nailed Him to the cross. Only our Lord, who has perfect knowledge about us, can still love us perfectly. There is nothing we need to hide from Him. We can talk openly and confess our

mistakes and failings to Him, knowing that He already knows them all, and yet He still loves us.

6. These Scriptures tell us that the revelation that marks a mature son or daughter of God is THE LORD OUR RIGHTEOUSNESS, which is also the revelation of the grace revolution. They clearly state that when Israel was a baby, God placed them under the law. But when Christ came, God placed all who believed in His Son under mature sonship. This tells us that in God's eyes, the law is basic; grace is maturity.

7. In Peter's early days with the Lord, he didn't understand Who the Lord was, and it was the *sense of His holiness* that he was most conscious of. But after Peter had walked with the Lord, he knew the Lord's heart and that the Lord had already forgiven him. It was the Lord's beautiful grace and love that gave Peter the courage to draw near to Him with full assurance of faith. Now, this is *true maturity—a growing revelation of His grace and forgiveness.*

SALVATION PRAYER

If you would like to receive all that Jesus has done for you and make Him your Lord and Savior, please pray this prayer:

Lord Jesus, thank You for loving me and dying for me on the cross. Your precious blood washes me clean of every sin. You are my Lord and my Savior, now and forever. I believe You rose from the dead and that You are alive today. Because of Your finished work, I am now a beloved child of God and heaven is my home. Thank You for giving me eternal life and filling my heart with Your peace and joy. Amen.

WE WOULD LIKE TO HEAR FROM YOU

If you have prayed the salvation prayer or if you have a testimony to share after reading this book, please send it to us via www.josephprince.com/testimony.

SPECIAL APPRECIATION

Special thanks and appreciation to all who have sent in their testimonies and praise reports to us. Kindly note that all testimonies are received in good faith and edited only for brevity and fluency. Names have been changed to protect the writers' privacy.

STAY CONNECTED WITH JOSEPH

Connect with Joseph through these social media channels and receive daily inspirational teachings:

Facebook.com/Josephprince
Twitter.com/Josephprince
Youtube.com/Josephprinceonline
Instagram: @JosephPrince

Free Daily E-mail Devotional
Sign up for Joseph's FREE daily e-mail devotional at JosephPrince.com/meditate and receive bite-size inspirations to help you grow in grace.

BOOKS BY JOSEPH PRINCE

GRACE REVOLUTION

Experience the revolution that is sweeping across the world! In *Grace Revolution*, Joseph Prince offers five powerful keys that will help you experience firsthand the grace revolution in your own life, and live above defeat. See how these keys can work easily for you, as you read inspiring stories of people who experienced amazing and lasting transformations when they encountered the real Jesus and heard the unadulterated gospel. Whatever your challenge today, begin to step away from defeat and take a massive leap toward your victory. Get your copy today and let the revolution begin in your life!

REIGN IN LIFE

Through ninety powerful inspirations that help you discover God's transforming grace, unleash His liberty and power to reign in all areas of life! When you reign, sin, sicknesses, addictions, and bondages don't. When you reign, God's provision, healing, wholeness, favor, and abundant life begin to manifest in your life. Let the truths of God's grace and the inspiring, personal stories of precious people transformed by His grace lead you to embark on your own journey of experiencing extraordinary breakthroughs.

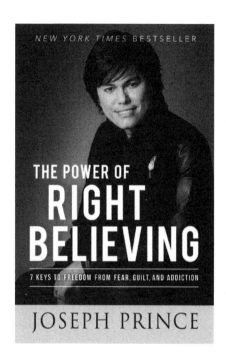

THE POWER OF RIGHT BELIEVING

Experience transformation, breakthroughs, and freedom today through the power of right believing! This book offers seven practical and powerful keys that will help you find freedom from all fears, guilt, and addictions. See these keys come alive in the many precious testimonies you will read from people around the world who have experienced breakthroughs and liberty from all kinds of bondages. Win the battle for your mind through understanding the powerful truths of God's Word and begin a journey of victorious living and unshakable confidence in God's love for you!

From *New York Times* Bestselling Author
JOSEPH PRINCE

100 DAYS
of
RIGHT
BELIEVING

Daily readings from *The Power of Right Believing*

A guide to help you live free
from fear, guilt, and addiction

100 DAYS OF RIGHT BELIEVING

What you believe is everything! When you begin to
believe right, the breakthroughs you want to see in your
life will manifest. With key teachings from *The Power of
Right Believing*, this hundred-day devotional aims to help
you develop highly effective habits for right believing that
will set you free from fears, guilt, addictions, and all kinds
of bondages. With faith-building Scriptures, prayers, and
powerful thoughts, these inspiring devotionals will lead
you to encounter God's love and grace afresh each day
and liberate you to live a life of joy and victory.

DESTINED TO REIGN

This pivotal and quintessential book on the grace of God will change your life forever! Join Joseph Prince as he unlocks foundational truths to understanding God's grace and how it alone sets you free to experience victory over every adversity, lack, and destructive habit that is limiting you today. Be uplifted and refreshed as you discover how reigning in life is all about Jesus and what He has already done for you. Start experiencing the success, wholeness, and victory that you were destined to enjoy!

UNMERITED FAVOR

This follow-up book to *Destined To Reign* is a must-read if you want to live out the dreams that God has birthed in your heart! Building on the foundational truths of God's grace laid out in *Destined To Reign*, *Unmerited Favor* takes you into a deeper understanding of the gift of righteousness that you have through the cross and how it gives you a supernatural ability to succeed in life. Packed with empowering new covenant truths, *Unmerited Favor* will set you free to soar above your challenges and lead an overcoming life as God's beloved today.

100 DAYS OF FAVOR

Dive headfirst into the vast ocean of God's favor and learn how it releases success in your life! Taking key teachings from *Unmerited Favor* and turning them into bite-size daily devotionals, Joseph Prince shows you how to develop favor-consciousness that releases the wisdom and blessings of God in everything you do, every day. With inspirational Scriptures, prayers, and liberating thoughts on God's unmerited favor in each devotional, *100 Days of Favor* is a must-have resource that will empower you to overcome every challenge in your life and walk in success.

NOTES

NOTES

NOTES